# What Others Are Saying

*True Worship vs. Strange Fire* answers many of the questions you might have had about worship. Patricia Taylor encourages you to have a greater receptiveness to hear, to understand, and to follow through with God's call. With spiritual profundity, she has written a book that brings down the "Glory Cloud." She has also highlighted practical applications of worship that will encourage you to develop a deeper intimacy with God.

**Bishop Joshua Smith, Ph.D.**
Chancellor; Professor of the Word of God International University; Overseer of the Word of God World Outreach

What is involved in truly worshiping God? Patricia Taylor says, "The purpose for gathering as the Body of Christ is to give God the glory and the adoration due His name. It is also a time to receive spiritual insight and instructions for our daily lives from the Word of God." In her book, *True Worship vs. Strange Fire*, you will be instructed on how to worship Him in spirit and in truth. Patricia will inspire you to deepen your intimacy with Him.

**Susan Titus Osborn**
Author of over 30 books

*True Worship vs. Strange Fire* is a book full of inspiration, instruction, faith challenges, and wisdom from the pages of God's Word and the life of a true worshiper. This book will inspire as well as serve as an excellent study guide.

**Dr. Diane Gardner**
#1 Best-Selling Author; Apostle; Pastor, Riverside, CA.


Patricia Taylor's book calls us into greater intimacy with God. She writes in a conversational way that makes her message simple yet profound. The truth she reveals is sensitive to the Holy Spirit and clearly biblical. For me, I found this book to be one that offers an "encounter" and not just another "how to" checklist.

**Kathleen D. Mailer**
Co-Founder of Iron Sharpens Iron Ministries (CANADA); #1 Best-Selling Author of over 50 books; Producer; Speaker; Founder of ChristianAuthorsGetPaid.com


Patricia Taylor has an infectious zeal for the Lord that permeates all that she does. She carries a powerful voice like a trumpet, heralding believers to their posts for spiritual battle. She possesses a tender heart of compassion that yearns to heal the wounded soul.

**Dr. Diane White-Clayton ("Dr. Dee")**
Choral Director, Faithful Central Bible Church, Inglewood, CA

In a time when "strange fire" has crept into the Church, Psalmist Patricia Taylor does an excellent job distinguishing, identifying, and exposing false worship while teaching, demonstrating, and restoring the pure worship Jesus deserves from His people. She is not just a worship leader but is also someone whom God has appointed in this new season as a lead worshiper to help lead others into the Holy of Holies to fully experience the glory of God. This is a must-read book.

**David and Joanna Hairabedian**
Founders of Virtual Church Media; Authors of more than 30 discipleship booklets and a multitude of video teachings

This powerful book reveals pure worship as reflected in Patricia's walk with the Lord, for when she sings, she puts it all on the altar, again and again. She will draw you deep into the holy presence of God through her worship.

**Diane Wendell, C.N.**
Naturopath; Nutritional Lifestyle Counselor

Patricia Taylor is a humble, mighty woman of God. She allows the Holy Spirit to guide her voice during worship and brings you into the very Throne Room of God. She is used tremendously to help war in the heavenlies with just the song that God has placed in her heart. This woman is on fire for Jesus, and wherever He sends her, she will set all within her proximity ABLAZE!

**Paul Ramos**
Paul Ramos Ministries

# True Worship
## VS.
# Strange Fire

A Journey to the Throne Room

SECOND EDITION

# PATRICIA TAYLOR

**True Worship vs. Strange Fire: A Journey to the Throne Room – Second Edition**
By Patricia Taylor
Copyright © 2021 by Patricia Taylor

Published by: Zapata
Website: patriciataylorministries.org
Email: patriciataylorministries@gmail.com

Cover design & Layout by: ChristianAuthorsGetPaid.com

Editor: Cheryl Regier & *Editing for Impact*
A Division of Zachariah House Inc.
www.Zachariah-House.com
zachariahhouseofhelps@gmail.com

Image in Chapter Eight created by: Joseph Devela

Printed in the United States of America
**ISBN 978-1-7923-6648-2**

#  Dedication

*I dedicate this book:*

To my daughter and son, Shonte and Travon,
who have inspired, encouraged, and prayed
for me to continue in my mandate from God,
and
to my wonderful grandchildren,
Te'Shon, Dealajuwon, Armon, TaNae, and Trevon.

*I also dedicate this book:*

To my cherished friend, Prophetess Elise Gatling,
who has supported and prayed for me
throughout the years.

*Finally, I dedicate this book:*

To all my readers,
who I pray will take a journey
into the Lord's presence
and experience an intimate relationship
with our Lord and Savior, Jesus Christ.

# Acknowledgments

I have learned that I can do all things through Christ who strengthens me. Writing this book was a challenging assignment, but I accomplished my goal with the help of the Holy Spirit and my supporters.

First and foremost, I thank my God, my Lord and Savior Jesus Christ, and the Holy Spirit for entrusting me to lead His people to joy and fulfillment in His presence through worship.

To my son, Travon Taylor, as well as to my son-in-law and daughter, LeNele and Asia Wiley... They consistently kept me in remembrance of my dream to write this book. I thank you for your faithful prayers and support.

To my best and dearest friend, Prophetess Elise Gatling... Thank you for your prophetic words, your prayers, and your support through the years and in this process.

To my editors of the first edition of this book, Susan Osborn and Ruth Yesmaniski... Thank you for your previous contributions into this project for God's glory.

To my editor, Cheryl Regier of Editing for Impact… Thank you so much for partnering with Holy Spirit to elevate my message and take this second edition to the next level.

A special acknowledgment and thank you goes out to Joseph Devela for the artistic rendering of the tabernacle featured in Chapter 8.

Thanks to my book mentor, Kathleen Mailer of ChristianAuthorsGetPaid.com, for lighting a spark under me, keeping me encouraged, and for teaching me how to develop and produce this book.

To all my supporters… THANK YOU!

I love you all!

# Table of Contents

# Foreword

Patricia has been a part of my worship team for years. When I first heard that she could sing, I asked her to sing during our Monday night service. When she opened her mouth, the people stood up and worshiped God. I saw an anointing on her, and I asked her if she realized how anointed she was.

Because of her anointing, I took her to Europe and around the country, and I observed the people worshiping. She also has worked for our ministry, praying for the partners. She is God's vessel of prayer and an instrument of worship.

I am excited that she has written this book, *True Worship vs. Strange Fire*. Patricia shares her intimate knowledge and understanding on how to enter into the Lord's presence through worship and how to recognize the counterfeit and fleshly, so-called worship.

*True Worship vs. Strange Fire* is more than just a book. It's an invitation, a journey, and a call for God's people to draw near to Him and become true worshipers. Through these pages, Patricia takes you on a journey, laying out the pathway to the presence of God. It is a practical guide to praise, intercession, and worship.

This book is helpful and full of quality material, and if followed, the principles expressed will keep an individual and the congregation in the power and presence of God, which is pleasing to Him.

I believe you will be blessed and draw nearer to our wonderful Lord while reading through the pages of this book. Enjoy the journey!

**Benny Hinn**
LoveWorld USA

# Introduction

Have you ever been invited to a church service but didn't experience worship there? I know that I have.

Most people think that worship is going through the rituals of the Sunday program at church. Each Sunday, the typical service includes listening to the choir or praise team sing two fast songs and a slow song for 15 minutes while the audience is invited to join in if they like. This is followed by announcements, the welcoming of visitors, words from the pastor, one or two offerings, and possibly an altar call for prayer. That is the extent of the standard worship service.

Many people limit the context of worship to time spent singing hymns and spiritual songs. Although music is appropriate and needed in church services, it is not all there is to worship. In addition, it is not just about going through the motions of simply singing a few songs each Sunday and calling that good enough.

For the most part, the Church has allowed our denominations to dictate how we worship. For example, in church services today, the music in each denomination has its own genre and its own artists. There is generally a selection of approved worship songs with lyrics along with some instrumental worship songs as well. It is all confined to what is deemed acceptable by the different denominations and its leadership.

Without true worship, though, we are just a bunch of churches full of religious and emotional congregants no matter what the denomination. Sadly, the Church as a whole along with many worship leaders and even some pastors do not understand the substance and depth of true worship. This kind of worship must be taught in such a way that the Church can fully engage in it and subsequently benefit from God's power operating through it and into their lives.

The purpose for gathering as the Body of Christ is to give God the glory and the adoration due His name. It is also a time to receive spiritual insight and instructions for our daily lives from the Word of God. Unfortunately, when our entire worship is reduced to what happens on a Sunday morning, we lose what worship is all about.

**Worship is a lifestyle.** It's *not* just for Sunday mornings. It is *not* just the singing and the praise. It is *not* just the sermon or anything else that is performed within the confines of a church building. It is a lifestyle, one that manifests a heart attitude towards God that is continuous and unceasing. We are to worship and glorify God *daily* and in *all* that we do.

My desire in writing this book is to teach you, the reader, how much our worship means to God. It really matters to Him! It matters that we worship Him in spirit and in truth.

4

Some questions for you to reflect on as you begin reading are:

- ➤ What is worship to me?
- ➤ How do I worship God?
- ➤ What kind of worshiper am I?
- ➤ Do I truly reverence Him?
- ➤ How well do I know Him?

Back in the Old Testament, God gave Moses a plan for building the Ark of the Covenant and the Tabernacle of God. This plan allowed God Himself to come down and dwell in the midst of His people. Through the rituals and sacrifices prescribed by God, the High Priest was able to come into the presence of the Almighty and represent the people. Each construction, each ritual, and each sacrifice had specific meaning with the intent of glorifying God and demonstrating what it meant to follow and reverence Him.

In a similar manner, my intent is to take you on a journey to the Throne Room so that you may experience the presence of the living God on a daily basis. On this journey, I will uncover what it means to have a heart of true worship before God. You will be instructed on how to worship Him in spirit and in truth as the Bible instructs. As a result, you will be inspired to deepen your intimacy with Him.

To God be the glory!

# CHAPTER ONE

## Strange Fire

One of the most powerful metaphors in the Bible is that of fire. Fire is a phenomenon common to all cultures and generations, and its practical and symbolic use represents many different meanings. In the Bible, it is used both literally and figuratively. It is generally related to some sort of manifestation of God's being or His action.

## The Fire of God

Here are some key manifestations of fire found in the Word and what they represent:

### 1. Fire communicates the very presence of God.

This was evident in the burning bush from which God spoke to Moses in Exodus 3:2-4:

*And the Angel of the Lord appeared to him in a flame of fire from the midst of a bush. So he looked, and behold, the bush was burning with fire, but the bush was not consumed. Then Moses said, "I will now turn aside and see this great sight, why the bush does not burn." So when the Lord saw that he turned aside to look, God called to him from the midst of the bush and said "Moses, Moses!" And he said, "Here I am."*

## 2. Fire is associated with God's glory.

Several passages in the Bible talk about God's glory manifesting through fire. For example, God's glory was seen by the Israelites at Sinai as we read about in Exodus 24:17:

*The sight of the glory of the Lord was like a consuming fire on the top of the mountain in the eyes of the children of Israel.*

## 3. Fire is a symbol of purity and the instrument of God's power.

Purification by fire demonstrates either destruction (judgment) or approval.

An example of purification through the fire of judgment was seen when Sodom and Gomorrah were destroyed with brimstone and fire from the Lord that poured out from Heaven in Genesis 19:24:

*Then the Lord rained brimstone and fire on Sodom and Gomorrah, from the Lord out of the heavens.*

Sodom and Gomorrah were two cities where the people lived wickedly sinful lives. An angel was sent to warn Lot to get out of the city along with his family before it was destroyed by God. After Lot and his family escaped, the Lord destroyed Sodom and Gomorrah with brimstone and fire that consumed those cities and all its people. The power of God purified the land of their wickedness through fire.

We see an example of the purifying fire that represents God's approval in 1 Peter 1:6-7:

> In this you greatly rejoice, though now for a little while, if need be, you have been grieved by various trials, that the genuineness of your faith, being much more precious than gold that perishes, though it is tested by fire, may be found to praise, honor, and glory at the revelation of Jesus Christ,

## 4. Fire represents the baptism of the Holy Spirit.

The New Testament imagery of fire is connected to the baptism of the Holy Spirit as John the Baptist predicted in Matthew 3:11:

> I indeed baptize you with water unto repentance, but He who is coming after me is mightier than I, whose sandals I am not worthy to carry. He will baptize you with the Holy Spirit and fire.

# What is strange fire?

Now that we have an understanding of what the fire of God looks like, what is the meaning of strange fire? First of all, the Hebrew word for strange is *zuwr*. Translated, it can mean a foreigner, a stranger, or an enemy. It can also refer to an adulteress or prostitute. Within this context, strange fire is a fire that is foreign and of enemy origin in that it prostitutes or profanes that which is meant to be holy and for the Lord.

To demonstrate the seriousness of strange fire, let's look at the story of Aaron and his sons...

Aaron and his sons were the chosen priests of God to serve in the tabernacle. Aaron, Moses's brother, was chosen as the first high priest of Israel. Aaron was married to Elisheba and had four sons: Nadab, Abihu, Eleazar, and Ithamar. Aaron and his sons were consecrated to their priestly office by Moses. (See Exodus 40:12-14) Their duty was to serve as priests for all of Israel.

Every day while the tabernacle was set up and the pillar of cloud or fire stood over the Holy of Holies where the Ark of the Covenant and the Mercy Seat were located, the Levites went about their duties of making sacrifices unto the Lord upon the altar. One of those sacrifices was called the burnt offering.

Leviticus 6:8-9a and 12-13 state:

> *Then the Lord spoke to Moses, saying, "Command Aaron and his sons, saying, 'This is the law of the burnt offering...*
>
> *'And the fire on the altar shall be kept burning on it; it shall not be put out. And the priest shall burn wood on it every morning, and lay the burnt offering in order on it; and he shall burn on it the fat of the peace offerings. A fire shall always be burning on the altar; it shall never go out.'*

Fire was commanded by God to constantly burn upon the altar. This continuous fire was a divinely appointed symbol and visible sign of the uninterrupted worship of Jehovah. It was a holy fire.

Aaron's sons, Nadab and Abihu, had been instructed by God through Moses on how they were to carry out their consecrated duties as priests. They were familiar with all the mandatory methods and ceremonies that had to accompany the different sacrifices upon the altar before God would accept it. They knew the dangers of not following God's ordained plan. Yet, it seemed like, for a brief and terrifying moment while doing their duties, they forgot how holy and righteous God was and how terrible His judgments could be.

Leviticus 10:1-3 tells us:

> *Then Nadab and Abihu, the sons of Aaron, each took his censer and put fire in it, put incense on it, and offered profane fire before the Lord, which He had not commanded them. So fire went out from the Lord and devoured them, and they died before the Lord. And Moses said to Aaron. "This is what the Lord spoke, saying: 'By those who come near Me I must be regarded as holy; And before all the people I must be glorified.'" So Aaron held his peace.*

Contrary to God's command, Nadab and Abihu each took their censers and brought fire from another source and offered this *"profane fire"* to the Lord as part of their service (worship) before the altar of God. Consequently, the Lord caused a fire to flare from His presence to burn them up, and the two men died as a result of their disobedience. God not only rejected their sacrifice, but He found it extremely offensive. Fire obtained from elsewhere is a strange fire.

Nadab and Abihu committed two distinct sins through their act. In the process of divine services, they did what was not commanded, for they:

1. Offered strange fire that was from their own making and not the holy fire of the altar before Jehovah. (v. 1)

2. Failed to sanctify themselves before Jehovah and the congregation. (v. 3)

In judgment of these two men for their strange fire, God made a point of instructing all the other priests who would serve in His tabernacle—His temple—as to what was holy versus unholy. Even we, the New Testament Church, have not been excluded, for it is imperative that we understand that our bodies act as God's temple. Therefore, we must not defile the temple of God.

Paul's states this very clearly in 1 Corinthians 3:16-17:

> *Do you not know that you are the temple of God and that the Spirit of God dwells in you? If anyone defiles the temple of God, God will destroy him. For the temple of God is holy, which temple you are.*

God did not want the disobedience of Nadab and Abihu to set a precedent for the future disregard of His commandments. We are a part of that future. We will face the judgment of God just as they did, and the glory of God will depart and leave us to our own devices IF we follow in their footsteps and offer strange fire.

Many believers may not identify with Nadab and Abihu, dismissing how their story is relevant to them today. Nevertheless, strange fire taints the Church even today. If we look closely, the inexcusable folly of these two men was in trying to please God "their way" instead of His way.

How many of us are guilty of doing "our own thing" or "saying what we want" and not obeying or saying what God says? How many of us continue to say, "I'll do it my way," and in so doing, defile our own temples?

The word 'Selah' in the Bible is sometimes interpreted to mean 'pause and think on what has just been said'. So, let's take a moment to reflect on how this directive applies to us today as it relates to what we offer unto the Lord.

If we preach a message that doesn't come from God, that is strange fire. If we take the liberty to prophesy, but it doesn't come from God, that is strange fire. If we try to fake worship or fake a shout, that is strange fire. If we do *anything* in the flesh, moving in our own strength and wisdom, that is strange fire. Believe it or not, our flesh can praise, it can sing, it can serve, it can worship falsely, and it sure can preach. What is seen or expressed on the outside doesn't always mean that it is holy and acceptable.

Many crafty, false preachers have infiltrated the Church, teaching what the people want to hear and not what God has said. There have been ministers who have exhibited unloving behavior, immoral and sensual lifestyles, and other conduct unbecoming of pastors and church leaders. These behaviors are another manifestation of strange fire and the defilement of God's temple.

Jude 1:4 (TLB) states:

*I say this because some godless teachers have wormed their way in among you, saying that after we become Christians we can do just as we like without fear of God's punishment. The fate of such people was written long ago, for they have turned against our only Master and Lord, Jesus Christ.*

There are many who have engaged in false worship, false praise, empty prayers, and unholy dancing. There are musicians playing unholy music and operating with no anointing, having no relationship with God. To them, their service to the Church is called a "gig." All this is strange fire.

Many "Christian" songs that are being sung today focus more on the problems and struggles we face rather than on the One who has all the answers. Then, when many of us hear a song that is closely related to our struggle, our emotions kick in. In response, we shout, dance, laugh, cry, and more, mistakenly thinking this is the Holy Spirit moving. Instead, it is feelings-based and not Spirit-driven. Worship songs are meant to be an anointed story, authored by the Spirit of God by way of our relationship with Him. When we allow our flesh to take over, though, it becomes strange fire.

# Consecration

In order to serve in the tabernacle, priests needed to be consecrated. As part of the consecration rituals, Moses sacrificed a ram of consecration. He took some blood from this ram and put it on the tip of Aaron's right ear, on the thumb of his right hand, and on the big toe of his right foot. He repeated that same ritual for each of Aaron's sons. (Exodus 29:20)

*Why* was blood applied to these particular extremities—the right ear, right hand, and right foot? I believe these parts signified that their whole spirit, soul, and body were to be consecrated to God and His service. Let's examine these three things a little more closely.

First, the blood was applied to the priest's right ear. **The ear symbolizes being able to hear from the Spirit of God and attend to His commands.** Today, preachers are often so busy doing church work that they don't spend time with the Lord to hear from Him. As a result, they preach the same warmed-over messages Sunday after Sunday, ones that tickle the congregation's ears. They have abandoned Spirit-led preaching to please their audience.

Pastors like this have turned their pulpit into a stage to achieve award-winning performances. Unfortunately, many congregations expect the performance. Unless the preacher is highly dramatic or adds background music to his preaching voice, runs around the church, or stands on the furniture, both the preacher and the people do not think he has preached. This is simply entertainment. God is not pleased!

God is looking for men and women who will diligently pursue Him and pray. He seeks men and women who choose to listen to and speak only what He has to say, bringing Spirit-inspired revelation to His people. God wants those who serve Him to carry His desire that all be saved and come to the knowledge of God. Their ears are tuned in to hear what the Spirit is saying. As Jesus said, *"He who has an ear, let him hear what the Spirit says to the churches..."* (Revelation 2:17a)

Next, the blood was applied to the priest's right thumb. **The thumb is a symbol of action, for it represents working with one's hands to perform the service to which God has called them to.** Every believer should make it his or her mission to grasp the things of God. Note that it's difficult to hold anything without a thumb. As believers, we must find our purpose in Christ and walk in it.

In addition, God is looking for those who have clean hands. In other words, their actions bear good fruit. They are the ones who will not lift themselves up in falsehood. They are the ones who become stronger and stronger in the will of God because they hold on to the Word and are not shaken. One with clean hands has a heart and soul that diligently pursues the things of God.

Next, the blood was applied to the right toe. **The toe symbolizes the pilgrimage of life.** Every believer, and especially preachers, should be able to stand firm in their faith and make progress on the dangerous path of testing and trouble. At the same time, we are to bring good tidings of great joy, publish peace, preach salvation, and teach with authority. We should not sway or go in the wrong direction, staying true to the Lord in our faith walk. Anyone who is anointed knows that *"The steps of a good man are ordered by the Lord, and He delights in his way."* (Psalms 37:23) God needs His children to not walk according to the flesh but according to the Spirit, their body a living sacrifice in their service unto Him.

## Reverential Fear

Nadab and Abihu were chosen by God. Their calling and election were sure. They were of the chosen few...and yet they disobeyed God's command. Their carelessness and irreverence were their downfall. Don't let this be said of us.

The seriousness of God's requirement on how to come before Him into His presence is clearly laid out for us in Scripture, especially with regard to reverential fear and praise. Let's examine the meaning of reverential fear for a clearer understanding.

The Hebrew word for fear is *yare.* It literally means 'to fear, be afraid, to revere, and to stand in awe, to have a deep respect or honor'. So, when we are told to fear God, we are commanded to have a deep, abiding respect for Him that includes a holy, reverential fear to honor Him.

Most often, this reverential fear is imparted when individuals encounter the Divine in the context of revelation. When God appears to a person, that person experiences the reality of God's holiness, and the fear of the Lord is birthed within. In return, God's work, power, majesty, and holiness evoke a godly fear that demands acknowledgment.

Reverential fear for who God is produces an awe that is seen in true worship. There is a mystery in divine holiness that causes individuals to become overwhelmed with a sense of admiration. In response, many people lift their hands in adoration, fall down before the Lord, or kneel in reverence. Others worship in song and through prayer. This devout fear leads to the confession of sins and the desire to earnestly seek God's will. Whatever the expression, those in awe of the God they serve gladly give Him the honor due His name through their worship.

The fear of God is not to be misunderstood as the dread that comes from the fear of punishment. In addition, it is not the kind of fear that makes the God we serve unapproachable or distant. Instead, it is the reverential regard, respect, and awe that comes out of our recognition and submission to the Divine.

In our current time, it doesn't seem as though the worship of God is approached with much degree of reverence. Many churches and church members treat their services as if they were simply a social event. Friends meet and visit during the service instead of paying attention to the sermon or engaging in praising God. Some sleep while others are constantly walking around. Others entertain thoughts of being somewhere else, or they are on their cell phones during the service, disrespecting God. Many come to church late every Sunday, distracting those who are worshiping and engaged. Is this the best we can offer God for all that He's done and is doing for us? Is just "showing up" good enough to be called worship?

Although we receive _from_ God when we come to church services, we are also to offer up something _to_ Him for all that He has done in our lives. So many have forgotten this. Instead, so many churches, besides being glorified social clubs, have become venues for entertainment, complete with singing, other performances, and emotionalism. There is no reverent fear of God. Although the outward appearance may look like pure worship, sadly, it is not.

God requires us to fear Him. This reverential fear includes us walking in all His ways—loving and serving Him with all our heart, soul, and mind. (Matthew 22:37) This is what it means to worship Him in spirit and in truth with a godly reverence that honors who He is and what He has done. (John 4:24)

As such, we must be careful not to worship God with our head and our intellect but worship Him with our heart. I am not saying this in judgment but out of observation. True worship is a heart expression birthed out of our reverential fear for God.

God knows our hearts—what we truly believe and our attitude towards Him. He seeks those who come to Him in humility, ready to sacrifice their pride and lay before Him humbly with a broken spirit and a contrite heart. (Psalms 51:17)

Reverential fear... It is an invitation to trust and obey. There is no other way.


## Set Apart

God spoke in Leviticus 20:7-8:

> *Consecrate yourselves therefore, and be holy, for I am the Lord your God. And you shall keep My statutes, and perform them: I am the Lord who sanctifies you.*

We have been set aside for God's holy purpose. Holiness is about being separated from everything profane and defiled and marked instead by a dedication to everything that is holy and pure. Therefore, as the Body of Christ, we cannot for the sake of our calling indulge in strange fire.

In 1 Peter 1:15-16 (AMPC), the Lord spoke again:

> *But as the One Who called you is holy, you yourselves also be holy in all your conduct and manner of living. For it is written, You shall be holy, for I am holy.*

We are to be holy and blameless—pure in heart. None but the pure in heart shall see God. In other words, there should be a God-like resemblance manifested through our conduct and manner of living, for we have been set apart for God to use. Therefore, as God's chosen people, we must consecrate ourselves to serving Him in the way that He has commanded.

Thank God for His grace and forgiveness and plenty of chances! We have ALL made mistakes in our worship before the Lord. Yet, because of His work on the cross, we can receive grace and forgiveness and begin afresh. His mercies are new every morning! Furthermore, it is by the blood of the Lamb that we are made holy in Him and not through our own strength and efforts. We have only to receive His gift of righteousness.

Nevertheless, we still must understand the seriousness of strange fire and choose to become a true worshiper of God. His grace and forgiveness are not a license to dismiss the importance of our worship before Him. Instead, His grace and forgiveness empower us to honor Him purposely and earnestly in worship.

If you are struggling in this area, ask God to create in you a clean heart and renew a right spirit within you. Ask Him to not cast you away from His presence or remove His Holy Spirit from you. Pray that He restores to you the joy of your salvation and upholds you by His Spirit. (Psalms 51:10-12) He *will* do it for His sake and because He loves you.

The command in Leviticus 20:7-8 to consecrate ourselves and be made holy comes with a promise. That promise is that the Lord WILL sanctify or purify us. That is what being set apart for His glory is all about.

# CHAPTER TWO

# Who Is God?

Successful Christian living begins with the knowledge of who God the Father is. It is difficult to be a true worshiper if you are not first acquainted with the Father.

The progressive revelation of God to His people in biblical times always involved a revelation of a name that described an eternal aspect of His divine nature. For example, God revealed Himself to Moses as the I AM THAT I AM in Exodus 3:14 (KJV). As New Testament Christians, we also need this revelation of the "I AM" presence of God. We must accept this revelation of God before we can come to Him.

The writer in Hebrews 11:6 declares:

> But without faith it is impossible to please Him, for he who comes to God must believe that He is, and that He is a rewarder of those who diligently seek Him.

We must exercise our faith to believe that God is who He says He is. Then as we seek Him, He will reveal to us the meaning of His names, giving us new insight into the magnificence of His character, for he longs to provide us with glimpses into the many facets of His glory and majesty.

Getting to know who God is involves communication. This includes prayer. Beginning in Matthew 6:9, we are given a model of how to pray. In that prayer, the first two words are *"Our Father..."* This opening greeting reveals a new dimension in our lives. We are no longer a solo act doing our own thing. Instead, we are now in a community, a fellowship that includes many brothers and sisters in the Lord who are seeking to communicate with Him. He is the One to whom we open our hearts, the One who has tender ears to hear His children who call His name.

The next portion of the model prayer is *"Hallowed be Your Name."* Hallowed is not a word that we use much anymore, yet the meaning is highly significant. It means 'to be made holy, to revere, to adore, respect, glorify, extol, honor, sanctify'. Being as worship is an expression of reverence and adoration where we honor and glorify the living God, when we hallow the Father in prayer, it is an act of worship that we give Him first.

Worshiping God attracts His benevolence and favor. His name is to be kept holy, by us and among us. As such, it is important to know the many aspects of His name in order to understand who He really is.

## The Father, Son, and Holy Ghost

There is only one "person" or one being who can be called God. There may be many gods in this world, but there is only one true

God. The term of "Father, Son, and Holy Ghost" refers to three manifestations of this one being—the Father who is the Creator of the world, the Son (Jesus) who is the Word that became flesh, and the Holy Ghost who was sent by Jesus as the Spirit of God to dwell within believers.

The Father, Son, and Holy Ghost are essential parts of one being in a similar manner as man is made up of spirit, soul, and body. Another way to look at it is through the roles each part takes. For example, I am a daughter to my parents, a sister to my siblings, a mother to my children, a grandparent to my grandkids, and so on and so forth. Yet, I am still "me" in one body, but each role defines or brings out a different aspect of who I am. Each aspect or characteristic makes up the whole.

God the Father—who Jesus called "Abba", meaning 'father'—is our sustainer and our source. You, too, can call Him Abba, and you can even call Him Daddy. Make it personal. Remember, this is a relationship between you and your Heavenly Father. He is the God who created and made you and called you by name.

Jesus the Son is the Messiah, our Savior. He came to earth to show us who the Father is and reveal to us what it means to be part of the family of God. Jesus is our friend.

The Holy Ghost or Holy Spirit is our Comforter. He was sent to bring further revelation of who God is and instruct us in how to live as children of the living God. The Holy Spirit is our teacher.

With this said, I would like to introduce you to other names of God and what they mean.

## The Names of God

God's names are dynamic. They are full of power. Through His names, God reveals great truths about Himself.

### 1. Elohim: God, Our Mighty Creator

Elohim is the primary Hebrew word for God in the Old Testament, and it appears in the first sentence of the Bible. The first part—El—means 'mighty' or 'strong'. Elohim is the plural form, and when referring to our Creator, it means 'God of gods'. This name is connected to power and supremacy. When we pray, we are remembering that He is the powerful One who began it all.

In Genesis 1:1, it states that *"In the beginning God created the heavens and the earth."* The record of Creation in Genesis recounts the details of the creation of the earth and the system (universe) to which the earth belongs as well as the creation of man. God was pleased with all that He had made, and we have the world and all its beauty to enjoy. Each day, we can find pleasure in Elohim's creativity and enjoy His glorious splendor.

Psalms 19:1 (AMPC) says, *"The heavens declare the glory of God; and the firmament shows and proclaims His handiwork."* Wherever we look, there is evidence of the greatness of Elohim, the mighty Creator. The heavens are the visible arch in which the clouds move. They celebrate and expose the splendor of God's handiwork. From sunrise to sunset, God's promises are revealed, and His knowledge and majesty are brought forth. How can anyone say there is no God when they witness His complex, intricate, and glorious creation each and every day and night?

## 2. El Roi: The God Who Sees

This name appears only once in the Bible in the story of Hagar's encounter with God in the desert. After Abram's wife, Sarai, had harshly mistreated her, Hagar fled from her. The angel of the Lord found her in the midst of her difficulties, and Hagar learned that El Roi was watching over her, and He had a plan to bless her and her son. In response, Hagar gave this name to the Lord who had spoken to her through the angel: *"You are the God who sees me," for she said, "I have now seen the One who sees me."* (Genesis 16:13, NIV)

One of God's attributes is that He is omniscient, which means that He is all-knowing. God is the one who numbers the hairs on our heads (Matthew 10:30) and who knows our circumstances— past, present, and future. When we pray to El Roi, we are praying to the One who knows and sees everything about us. There is comfort in knowing that God is conscious of and cares about every detail of our lives.

Another attribute of God is that He is omnipresent, which means He's everywhere and is always present. When you are mistreated, abused, or used, God knows and sees everything and is there for you and ready to help. As Solomon declared in Proverbs 15:3, *"The eyes of the Lord are in every place, keeping watch on the evil and the good."*

### 3. El Shaddai: God Almighty

Our God is the God Almighty—El Shaddai. He can handle any situation because He is Almighty and all-sufficient. Nobody is stronger than He. Nobody is more powerful than He. He can do anything and everything necessary to look after us. El Shaddai is able to meet all our needs, and He will fulfill His promises to us in His perfect time and way. What seems impossible to us is more than possible for Him, for nothing is impossible for God.

When we pray to El Shaddai, we invoke the name of the One for whom nothing is impossible. As Jesus said in Matthew 19:26, *"With men this is impossible, but with God all things are possible."*

God is also omnipotent, which means He has all power. In other words, He is the Almighty. There is nothing that He cannot do, for He has the divine ability to subdue all things. As Jeremiah acknowledged in Jeremiah 32:17, *"'Ah, Lord God! Behold, You have made the heavens and the earth by Your great power and outstretched arm. There is nothing too hard for You.'"* Indeed, all power belongs to Him!

God being omnipotent is the most misunderstood attribute. Unbelievers who have heard that He has all power accuse Him of not using His power to keep bad things from happening. What they don't understand is that God chose to allow His power to be limited through *the power of choice He gave us* (free will). Yet be assured, God will one day put an end to evil once and for all. Because of His great mercy before that great Judgment Day, He allows us to choose between His Kingdom or the kingdom of Satan. By extension, this allows us to make choices regarding our destinies.

It is a wonderful security to know that we serve an all-powerful God of love. It is a blessing to know that our eternal safety lies in the strength of our relationship with Him, our El Shaddai.

## 4. El Elyon: God Most High

The term Elyon means 'Highest' or 'Exalted One'. This name emphasizes that God is the highest in every realm of life. He is Sovereign Ruler over all the universe.

All who belong to Christ are revealed to be sons and daughters of the Most High through their reflection of the Father in Heaven. Jesus, Himself, is known as the Son of the Most High. As He stated in John 14:9, *"He who has seen me has seen the Father"*. As the Son of God, He reflects the image of who the Most High is.

The Holy Spirit is known as the power of the Most High. In Luke 1:35 when the angel announced to Mary that she was to bear the Messiah, the angel said, *"The Holy Spirit will come on you, and the power of the Most High will overshadow you."* (NIV) This same Holy Spirit is what was given to the Church upon Jesus' ascension into Heaven, a gift that reflects the Most High.

Therefore, when we praise and worship the Most High, we are praising and worshiping the One whose power, mercy, and sovereignty cannot be matched.

### 5. Adonai: Lord and Master

This Hebrew word of *Adonai* means 'My Lord'. It also means 'ruler, master, king'. God is Lord and Master, our Adonai.

Adonai is a name that implies relationship, for we are His servants. As we pray to Adonai, we must surrender every aspect of our life to Him, praying that His grace will make us the kind of servants who are quick to do His will. This relationship comes with a special promise as we read about in Psalms 16:2 (NLT) where it says, *"I said to the Lord, 'You are my Master! Every good thing I have comes from you.'"*

We must remember that the Lord is the only One who can empower us to fulfill His purposes through our lives. In fact, it is in knowing Him as Adonai that we discover a true sense of purpose and direction.

## 6. Jehovah

Jehovah means 'self-existent One' or 'He brings into existence whatever exists'. Jehovah is God, the One who is both self-existent and eternal.

Another word for Jehovah is Yahweh or YHWH according to the Hebrew Bible. This name for God was regarded by the Jews as too sacred to be spoken.

Jehovah is the name that represents covenant relationship. Covenant relationship implies a special kinship, family tie, blood tie, or intimacy. This covenant involves all the promises of God towards His people, the agreement He makes with His children to be faithful as Jehovah God. This relationship is what it's all about.

Jehovah expresses personality, for He is the source of living. He is never called "living Jehovah." Rather, He is LIFE itself. As Paul said in Acts 17:28, *"for in him we live and move and have our being, as also some of your own poets have said, 'For we are also His offspring.'"* Jehovah is connected to man in that He is the One who formed man from the dust of the ground, breathing His life into all of humanity.

God introduced Himself to Moses as Jehovah when he voiced, *"I AM THAT I AM"*. (Exodus 3:14, KJV) He is an endless presence, for He doesn't just exist—He IS existence. As Jehovah, He brings healing, restoration, provision, sanctification, righteousness, protection, peace, and much more. He is the All in All, an all-pervasive presence who desires to be in relationship with His chosen people.

Whatever your status in life, God wants you to know Him. He longs for you to enter into this intimate covenant of love with Him. It's an ongoing relationship that will continue throughout generations.

### 7. Jehovah-Jireh: The Lord Will Provide

The word Jireh means 'to see', and to see means 'vision'. Provide is taken from two Latin words *pro-* meaning 'first' or 'before', and *videre* meaning 'to see'. Together, *providere* in Latin means to 'foresee' and 'attend to'.

God sees and provides for His children. He knows what His children need and promises to supply everything that is necessary for us to live a godly life. God sees into the future as well as knows the past and the present. He anticipates and attends to what is needed in the days ahead. He will give us what we need…always. We have only to receive.

In Genesis 22:8-14, it says:

> *And Abraham said, "My son, God will provide for Himself the lamb for a burnt offering." So the two of them went together.*

*Then they came to the place of which God had told him. And Abraham built an altar there and placed the wood in order; and he bound Isaac his son and laid him on the altar, upon the wood. And Abraham stretched out his hand and took the knife to slay his son.*

*But the Angel of the Lord called to him from heaven and said, "Abraham, Abraham!" So he said, "Here I am."*

*And He said, "Do not lay your hand on the lad, or do anything to him; for now I know that you fear God, since you have not withheld your son, your only son, from Me."*

*Then Abraham lifted his eyes and looked, and there behind him was a ram caught in a thicket by its horns. So Abraham went and took the ram, and offered it up for a burnt offering instead of his son.*

*And Abraham called the name of the place, The-Lord-Will-Provide; as it is said to this day, "In the Mount of the Lord it shall be provided."*

When we pray to Jehovah-Jireh, we are praying to the God who sees the situation, whatever it might be, and has a plan in place to provide for our every need, whatever the need may be. God is our Source for all provision, both now and into the future.

## 8. Jehovah-Nissi: The Lord Is My Banner

In Exodus 17:8-16, we read how Amalek came and fought against Israel. There was to be no flag of surrender in this battle, for God was very clear that they were to *"fight with Amalek."* (v. 9) Why? Because Amalek and his people, who were descendants of Esau, were enemies of God, and they had to be subdued even if it meant war. After this battle against Amalek, God was worshiped as Jehovah-Nissi for the first time because it was His banner that was raised in victory over the enemy.

Through this event, God demonstrates to us a great principle for attaining victory over our enemy—Satan and his demonic forces, the flesh, etc. The Bible tells us that God is the commanding officer of the hosts of Heaven, the leader of the army of the Almighty. He is always victorious, always triumphant, and always the winner! Thus, He is our banner—our standard, covering, protection, and victory. He overcomes evil. His truth and goodness will prevail, and we will live as more than conquerors because of what He has done for us. When you pray to Jehovah-Nissi, you are praying to the God who is powerful enough to overcome any enemy.

## 9. Jehovah-Rapha: The Lord Who Heals

The Hebrew word *rapha* means 'to heal, cure, restore, or make whole'. Shortly after the children of Israel left Egypt and were headed to the Promised Land, God revealed Himself as Jehovah-Rapha, their Healer.

Exodus 15:26 (NLV) states:

*He said, "Listen well to the voice of the Lord your God. Do what is right in His eyes. Listen to what He tells you, and obey all His Laws. If you do this, I will put none of the diseases on you which I have put on the Egyptians. For I am the Lord Who heals you."*

God is a good God. He desires only the best for us. He is our Covenant Healer. As part of that covenant, He has placed two conditions before His people.

First, God asks us to *"listen well"* to His voice. As God speaks, we must cultivate an attitude of listening for His voice. He speaks in many ways—through His Word, His anointed servants, and direct revelation to our inner man. He is seeking all those who will listen to Him.

Second, God asks us to *"do what is right in His eyes."* Not only does God want us to listen to His voice, but He wants us to heed His Word and be obedient to that Word. Through our obedience, He heals, cures, restores, repairs, and mends our physical bodies, heals our soul, and restores our spiritual condition.

As you pray, ask God to search your heart. Take time to let Him show you what it contains and uncover any hidden sin. Repent and ask for forgiveness. Then, petition your Jehovah-Rapha to heal all your infirmities. As Psalms 107:20 promises, *"He sent*

His word and healed them, and delivered them from their destructions."

If you are sick in your body, remember, Jesus bore your sickness and carried your pain. Therefore, give no place to sickness or pain. However, when you pray it must come from a knowing that healing is already available to you. Your prayer must come from your heart and not from your head.

## 10. Jehovah-Shalom: The Lord Is Peace

Judges 6:24 states:

*So Gideon built an altar there to the Lord, and called it The-Lord-Is-Peace. To this day it is still in Ophrah of the Abiezrites.*

The English definition of peace generally refers to the absence of outward conflict or to a state of inner calm. However, the Hebrew word for peace—*shalom*—includes 'wholeness, completeness, finished word, perfection, safety', and 'wellness'. This understanding of peace takes inner calm to a whole new level.

This *shalom* peace comes from living in harmony with God. The fruit of that harmony is harmony with others, prosperity, health, satisfaction, soundness, wholeness, and well-being. When we submit to Him and live as He calls us to, we experience peace even when everything around us is in chaos.

True peace implies that nothing is missing, nothing is broken. It doesn't mean freedom from commotion, but it does mean we're safe. We can fully experience God's benefits (which includes success and happiness) despite what is going around us. It means we can experience prosperity physically, mentally, financially, and spiritually. *Shalom* is a deep, inner peace that supersedes everything external and allows us to function and prosper from a place of God's favor and rest.

Isaiah 26:3 (AMPC) says:

*You will guard him and keep him in perfect and constant peace whose mind [both its inclination and its character] is stayed on You, because he commits himself to You, leans on You, and hopes confidently in You.*

Lay all your worries and concerns at His feet, and you will experience His peace that passes all understanding. (See Philippians 4:7) When we pray, we are praying to the source of lasting inner peace.

## 11. Jehovah-Tsidkenu: The Lord Our Righteousness

Righteousness is not a popular word in our culture. Yet, it is essential to our joy because it involves being in right relationship or right standing with God and conforming to His character, fulfilling our responsibilities toward Him and others.

Jeremiah 23:6 says:

> *In His days Judah will be saved, and Israel will dwell*
> *safely; Now this is His name by which He will be called:*
> *THE LORD OUR RIGHTEOUSNESS.*

God is upright, just, and holy. But the greatest wonder of all is that He has made it possible for us to be holy also. No matter how hard we try, we will always fall short of the perfection of God. Still, He loves us so much that He doesn't want to live without us. That is why He sent Jesus to make a way for us to become righteous.

Those who have given their lives to Christ have been justified. In other words, we have been declared and made righteous by God through the blood of Jesus. Anyone who accepts Jesus as their Lord and Savior and lives according to the Word is in right standing with the Father. It is our relationship with Him through Jesus Christ that establishes our position as the righteous.

When we pray to our Jehovah-Tsidkenu, we are praying to the One who has intervened on our behalf to restore us to His likeness—made holy and righteous. Therefore, as the righteous, we are restored to right fellowship with Him.

### 12. Jehovah-Rohi: The Lord Is My Shepherd

We have the blessings of the Good Shepherd who is the God of grace and compassion.

In Psalms 23:1, we read:

*"The Lord is my shepherd; I shall not want."*

This means that He is always dependable, always faithful, and always constant. We can count on Him to come through for us—always protecting us, providing for us, guiding us, and leading us to safety.

With His rod, He fights off our enemy, and with His staff, He gently leads us along the paths of righteousness. He will even come after us if we stray. What joy it is to know that He nurtures us, loves us, and provides for us always.

Our Jehovah-Rohi watches over us day and night, feeding us and leading us with love and care and our best interests in mind. We can commit our needs into the Good Shepherd's hands with confidence in His care.

## 13. Jehovah-Mekaddishkem: The Lord Who Sanctifies

Leviticus 20:8 gives us a clearer meaning of this name. It reads, *"And you shall keep My statutes, and perform them: I am the Lord who sanctifies you."* The Lord is our sanctifier.

The dominant idea of sanctification is being separated from the secular and sinful lifestyle in exchange for a life that is holy. In other words, sanctification sets us apart for a sacred purpose.

We are called upon to be holy and obedient to God's commands. We are set apart for His use. Therefore, we must surrender to the will of Jehovah-Mekaddishkem who sanctifies us for His purposes. He readily accepts us, forgives us, and cleanses us, transforming us for service.

Jesus said in His prayer in John 17:19 (AMPC):

> And so for their sake and on their behalf I sanctify (dedicate, consecrate) Myself, that they also may be sanctified (dedicated, consecrated, made holy) in the Truth.

Sanctification is a lifelong process that involves us making a choice to allow God to set us apart from the world for His divine use. This allows us to fulfill His plans and purpose for our lives.

Sanctification also enables us to become more intimate with God because it draws us away from sin and focuses our attention on the Heavenly Father. Through its transforming power, we are conformed to the image of His Son, Jesus. Only holiness can abide in the presence of the Most Holy God. Therefore, holiness is not an option but a requirement. Thus, we need to be sanctified.

In Psalms 51:7, it says, *"Purify me with hyssop, and I shall be clean…"* (AMPC) Hyssop is an herb associated with cleansing and purification. It symbolizes a purging of all the filth of sin through the blood sacrifice of Jesus.

Therefore, if you desire a thorough cleansing from the sin nature, ask the Lord, your Jehovah-Mekaddishkem, to do so. You can start with this prayer from Psalms 51:7-12:

*Purge me with hyssop, and I shall be clean; Wash me, and I shall be whiter than snow. Make me hear joy and gladness, that the bones You have broken may rejoice. Hide Your face from my sins, and blot out all my iniquities. Create in me a clean heart, O God, and renew a steadfast spirit within me. Do not cast me away from Your presence, and do not take Your Holy Spirit from me. Restore to me the joy of Your salvation, and uphold me by Your generous Spirit.*

### 14. Jehovah-Shammah: The Lord Is There

Shammah is actually the name of a city. However, this name is so closely associated with God's presence and power—His omnipresence—that it is also viewed as one of the names of God. Specifically, this name for God is associated with the restoration of Jerusalem, God's dwelling place, as we read about in Ezekiel 48. As Ezekiel 48:35b states, *"...and the name of the city from that day shall be: THE LORD IS THERE."*

God desires to dwell with us always, just as He desired to dwell with Israel. To that end, He clothed Himself in humanity through His Son, Jesus, making a way for us to reside together with Him for all eternity. Then, through the sending of the Holy Spirit, He abides with us continuously. If the Holy Spirit does not dwell within us, we do not belong to Him.

God promises that He will never leave us or forsake us. He has spoken the Word, and He cannot lie. He is the "Lord Who Is There" whether we feel Him there or not. He will be a divine presence in the time of trouble. He is Jehovah-Shammah.

It is only through the hallowing, in being set apart, and in praising God that we experience greater levels of confidence in who He is and His ability to bring us from a place of insufficiency to a land of peace, prosperity, and abundance. God dwells with those that fear (reverence) Him.

Although there are other names in the Bible that describe God's character, attributes, and revelation, the ones that I have given you will, through your meditation and prayers, lead you to the Throne Room to worship Him in spirit and in truth.

I encourage you to pray and ask God to give you further insight into each one of these names. Study the Scriptures and ask Him to teach you about His character and attributes. Also, ask Him to show you what each characteristic means for you personally and how to apply the power of His names in your life. Use His names to cry out to Him for every need. Now, thank Him And praise Him, for He alone is worthy!

*Give unto the Lord*
*the glory due to His name;*
*Worship the Lord*
*in the beauty of holiness.*

Psalms 29:2

# CHAPTER THREE

## Call on the Name of Jesus

First, let's establish who Jesus is...

Jesus is the ultimate revelation of God the Father as His Son. He is the promised Messiah and Savior of the world. The Greek translation of the Hebrew name of *Jeshua* means 'He shall save'. Before He was born of the Virgin Mary, He was affirmed in the Old Testament as we read about in Psalms 2:7, which says, *"I will declare the decree: The Lord has said to Me, 'You are My Son, today I have begotten You.'"*

Jesus was in the beginning before the beginning began. His pre-existence is documented in Proverbs 8:22-31 (NLT):

*"The Lord formed me from the beginning, before he created anything else. I was appointed in ages past, at the very first, before the earth began. I was born before the oceans were created, before the springs bubbled forth their waters. Before the mountains were formed, before the hills, I was born—before he had made the earth and fields and the first handfuls of soil. I was there when he established the heavens, when he drew the horizon on the oceans. I was there when he set the clouds above, when he established springs deep in the earth.*

*I was there when he set the limits of the seas, so they would not spread beyond their boundaries. And when he marked off the earth's foundations, I was the architect at his side. I was his constant delight, rejoicing always in his presence. And how happy I was with the world he created; how I rejoiced with the human family!"*

The Gospel of John also talks about the pre-existence of Jesus. In chapter 1 and verse 1, we read that *"In the beginning the Word already existed. The Word was with God, and the Word was God."* (NLT) Then, in verse 14, John goes on to say that *"...the Word became flesh and dwelt among us, and we beheld His glory, the glory as of the only begotten of the Father, full of grace and truth."*

In the Greek, 'word' as it appears in these two verses is defined as *logos*. *Logos* means 'divine utterance', plus it is 'the thought, the expression, the truth, the knowledge, the intent', and 'the wisdom of God'. Jesus was and is the eternal Word that was made flesh.

Everything about Christianity is determined by the person and work of Jesus Christ. In every detail, Christianity owes its life, substance, and character to Christ, the Anointed One. He is the author of its teachings. He is the object of its doctrine. He is the origin of its salvation. He is the fulfillment of its hopes. He is the source of its power. He is the founder of its Church. In addition to all this, He is the One who gave us the Holy Spirit as a legacy to those who believe. Jesus is the eternal and ultimate expression of God.

I believe that we all need a fresh revelation of how big our Lord and Savior is. More often than not, our view or understanding of Christ is much too small. Consequently, we may feel unwilling to allow Him to have any authority or control much less outright ownership of our lives. Having a deeper appreciation of the greatness of who Jesus is opens the door to the blessings of living a life of complete surrender.

The reality of the person of Jesus Christ must be the center of everything. Church should be about Jesus, the One who purchased it with His blood. Worship should be about the One who is worthy of worship. Prayer should be about the God we pray to in the name of Jesus.

The Father's love was demonstrated through the sending of His Son. Jesus is a real person, which means you and I can know Him and love Him. Loving Him is life's greatest achievement and the highest calling.

If you want to fall in love with Jesus again, allow the Spirit of God to take you by the hand and place you at the feet of Jesus. He longs for you to love Him and know Him intimately. My prayer is that He will take you back to where it all began when you first believed.

# Call on His Name

It is important to study and come to know the many facets or characteristics of who Jesus really is. This will help us to grasp the expansiveness of who He is for us and in us. Our worship of Him will increase when we become intimately acquainted with Him. Calling on His name is all about relationship.

## 1. The Only Begotten Son of the Father, Our Savior

We established in the beginning of this chapter who Jesus is. He was God who became flesh. This is one of the most sublime statements in all of Scripture. Jesus Christ was the physical manifestation of love on earth, the only Begotten Son of the Father.

Jesus is the most unique figure in the world's history. He was God, holy and divine. Yet, He humbled Himself to become a man—a man who was sinless, the perfect one. Great is this mystery of godliness, where God manifested Himself in the flesh. He was wholly God, able to forgive sin, and wholly man, sent to atone for sin. So, this God-man is our Savior. Oh, come let us worship and adore Him!

## 2. Faithful and True

I looked all over and couldn't find anyone I could apply these attributes to but to Jesus. In fact, in Revelation 19:11, Jesus Christ is identified by the name *"Faithful and True"*. He is the only One who is always faithful and true to His promises. He is completely trustworthy and true to His Word.

The Word of God says in 2 Corinthians 1:20:

> For all the promises of God in Him are Yes, and in Him Amen, to the glory of God through us.

There is no change in who God is. He's the same yesterday, today, and forever as we read about in Hebrews 13:8. His promises are always "yes," and in Him, they are always truthful. Not one promise of God is a "no" to the one who believes and meets the conditions. By His Spirit, He has stamped us with His eternal pledge.

When you pray, tell the Lord that you believe in Him and His Word and that you will meditate on it day and night. Ask Him to restore the joy of your salvation and keep you faithful and true.

### 3. Bread of Life

In John 6:35 and verses 48-51, we read:

> And Jesus said to them, "I am the bread of life. He who comes to Me shall never hunger, and he who believes in Me shall never thirst.

> I am the bread of life. Your fathers ate the manna in the wilderness, and are dead. This is the bread which comes down from heaven, that one may eat of it and not die. I

*am the living bread which came down from heaven. If anyone eats of this bread, he will live forever; and the bread that I shall give is My flesh, which I shall give for the life of the world."*

Jesus is the real heavenly bread—the true, life-sustaining power given to the world. Anything else, regardless of its religious significance in the past or present, is an inadequate substitute. As the Bread of Life, Jesus is the Life-giver.

How is this bread to be dispensed? It must be made known to an ignorant world!

In today's society, we are so easily caught up with the world's cheap bread. Cheap bread comes in many forms such as money, success, comfort, and pleasures that we indulge in and rely on, effectively taking the edge off our spiritual hunger. In doing so, we fail to realize the dangers of living in an affluent, consumer-driven society in which we are often consumed by the things we desire. So many of us are like sponges, soaking up the world's good things but leaving no space for God.

If your spiritual life seems dull, it may well be that you've been focused on consuming the cheap bread of the world. Ask Jesus for the grace to seek Him first, to feast on His living bread by which you will never hunger again. Ask Him to show you how to feed on Him—His life, His sacrifice, His Word, and His promises. I guarantee, you will be satisfied for life!

### 4. Light of the World

Another name for Jesus is "Light of the World." John 8:12 tells us this:

> Then Jesus spoke to them again, saying, "I am the light of the world. He who follows Me shall not walk in darkness, but have the light of life."

John's gospel portrays Jesus as the light that vanquishes the gloom and darkness brought on by sin that leads to death. If we follow Him—our Light—we shall not walk in darkness.

1 John 1:7 states:

> But if we walk in the light as He is in the light, we have fellowship with one another, and the blood of Jesus Christ His Son cleanses us from all sin.

Jesus is manifested as the Light of the World through the lives of His children. We are encouraged to walk as children of Light because we were once in darkness ourselves. We must also realize that our lives have either a positive or negative effect on those with whom we are in contact. It is imperative that we always live responsibly to bring glory to God.

If you know that your light is dim, confess any alliance with darkness. Ask God to help you walk in obedience to bring His Light back into your life so that your life may shine brightly and reflect God's glory.

## 5.  The Good Shepherd

Jesus tells us in John 10:11:

*"I am the good shepherd. The good shepherd gives His life for the sheep."*

Many people are desperate for guidance, searching for ways to navigate through life. Throughout this process, confusion often fills one's mind. This makes decisions incredibly difficult.

In trying to seek answers for the never-ending questions in our lives, many of us look for those answers in books, through seminars, and from various professionals and experts just to name a few. We may even spend thousands of dollars in our quest for answers. However, the true answer to all our questions lies with the Shepherd who has been guiding people since the dawn of creation.

The Bible also describes Him as the Chief Shepherd in 1 Peter 5:4. With that in mind, I want to impress upon you that God is good, and Jesus is God. What is the responsibility of the Good Shepherd—our God, Jesus Christ? He meets every need. He lets us rest. He leads us to peaceful streams. He renews our strength. He guides us into right paths. He protects and comforts us. He prepares a feast for us. He anoints our head with oil. He pursues us with an unfailing love, and He blesses us. *This* is our Good Shepherd.

Stop for a few moments to sense His presence. His wonderful eyes are fixed on *you*. His holy desire is to draw you lovingly to Himself, for He's longing to speak to you. Listen to Him! He cares for YOU.

## 6. Immanuel or Emmanuel

Matthew 1:22-23 states that:

> *So all this was done that it might be fulfilled which was spoken by the Lord through the prophet, saying: "Behold, the virgin shall be with child, and bear a Son, and they shall call His name Immanuel," which is translated, "God with us."*

The name Immanuel appears in the Old Testament two times (Isaiah 7:14; 8:8) and once in the New Testament as we see above. Depending on the Bible translation, this name of the Lord is sometimes spelled as Emmanuel. Both are Messianic names that mean 'God with us'.

When our sins made it impossible for us to come to Him, God took the extraordinary step of coming to us by sending His Son to redeem us from our sins. Our Immanuel came to earth, made Himself susceptible to sorrow, exposed Himself to temptation, and became vulnerable to sin's disruptive power...*yet He knew no sin*. He did this to cancel sin's claim and make a way for us to have direct access to God once again.

In Jesus, we see how extreme God's love is through the steps He took to reconcile us to Himself so that we could be with Him as He is with us. Remember this the next time you feel discouraged, abandoned, or too timid to undertake some new endeavor. Remember that Jesus is still Immanuel today. He is still "God with us."

One of the greatest promises in the Bible is found in Matthew 28:20. To capture the depth of this promise, I will be quoting from the AMPC version. It says:

> Teaching them to observe everything that I have commanded you, and behold, I am with you all the days (perpetually, uniformly, and on every occasion), to the [very] close and consummation of the age. Amen (so let it be).

If the Lord is with us always and in all ways, what do we have to fear? How can we lose? This same Lord who walked on water, healed the sick, and rose from the dead watches over us continuously, ready to guide and help us. Why do we sometimes act as if God is not anywhere in the vicinity?

There may be many reasons why we feel like God is absent in our lives. One reason might be that our spiritual sensors are not working too well. However, a more common reason is that we are the ones who go AWOL, not God. When we allow sin or other distractors to drag us down and/or pull us away from the One who has promised to be with us, we give in to the temptation to run from Him instead of running to Him. At this point, we find it hard to pray let alone worship.

If you have found yourself in trouble by some persistent failing of by some entrenched sin, don't run away from Jesus. Instead, express your sorrow and ask for His forgiveness. He *will* forgive you. Now, praise God for His promise to be with you.

## 7. The Great I Am

The first time we see this name is in Exodus 3:13-14:

> *Then Moses said to God, "Indeed, when I come to the children of Israel and say to them, 'The God of your fathers has sent me to you,' and they say to me, 'What is His name?' what shall I say to them?"*

> *And God said to Moses, "I AM WHO I AM." And He said, "Thus you shall say to the children of Israel, 'I AM has sent me to you.'"*

God's response was not a "name" that makes God an object of definition or limitation. Rather, it was an affirmation that God IS, and He is always free to be and act as He wills. He is the Almighty, the Absolute, the Infinite, and the All-sufficient God.

In the New Testament, recognition is given to Jesus as "I Am". He is one in word and action with the Father. Jesus is the "I Am" who was, who is, and who is to come. "I Am" is whatever you need Him to be, not in the worldly sense but according to the

Word. For example, He is courage in your difficulties, strength in your weakness, joy in your sorrow, and victory over your enemies. He is mercy, grace, and a God who forgives you when you miss the mark. He is ever present even in times of trouble. He IS the Great I AM!

## 8. The Way, the Truth, and the Life

In John 14:6, we read:

> *Jesus said to him, "I am the way, the truth, and the life.*
> *No one comes to the Father except through Me."*

Jesus is the Way. He is the straight and narrow Way, the only Way that leads directly to the Father. When we walk in the Way, we walk in Light, for the Way is lit by His countenance. He holds us by the hand and supplies our every need for life as the beloved. He has made the way for us to journey with Him in sweet fellowship. What a Savior! What a joyful journey!

He is not only the Way and the Truth, but He is also the Life. He is Eternal Life, the Author of Life, the Giver of Life, and the Source of Life. He left Heaven and the throne of God, coming to this earth to secure everlasting life for us. He came to reveal Himself as the Life that He might receive to Himself those who were (and are) to inherit through Him and share with Him this eternal life. Our pilgrimage here is short in all reality and will soon be ended. Then... Oh, what joy! We will enter the unending LIFE that is found in our Savior! Praise Him!

## 9. The Truth

Jesus is the Truth without any contradiction. As the Truth, He is reliable and can be trusted. Everyone who is born of God listens to the Truth. As a result, we walk as God's free people, for we know Him who is the Truth, and it is Truth that makes us free. His truth is the greatest gift of life, and if we love Him, we will exercise that truth.

John 1:17 states:

> For the law was given through Moses, but grace and truth came through Jesus Christ.

No one has ever seen God. Yet, Jesus was born and came into the world to testify to the truth of who He is. It was Jesus—the Son who was close to the Father's heart—who has made Him known in all truth.

We must pray for those who preach and teach strange fire in our churches. We must intercede for those whose teachings and guidance deflect believers away from the Word of God to which Jesus has set His eternal seal. For those who are deceived, we need to pray that they have a fresh revelation of the Truth so that they can repent and follow the Way with no compromise.

Jesus is the keeper of all truth! Ask the Holy Spirit to lead you in all truth and teach you. Thank the Lord Jesus Christ, for He is the God of your salvation. He is the Truth!

## 10. The True Vine

Christ is the True Vine, and the Father is the Husbandman. Every believer in Christ is referred to as the branch according to John 15:1-2:

> *"I am the true vine, and My Father is the vinedresser. Every branch in Me that does not bear fruit He takes away; and every branch that bears fruit He prunes, that it may bear more fruit."*

If a believer is to remain fruitful, they are pruned to produce more fruit. This often involves purging that which is not conducive to growth and righteous living. If a believer is fruitless, they are taken away or removed from being part of the Vine. The Father does this, not man. Producing fruit is a mandate for all believers.

He is the True Vine in which we abide, bearing fruit for God's kingdom. We cannot bear fruit on our own. Abiding in the Word helps us to produce good fruit. As such, we must continue to deepen our relationship with Jesus Christ who is the Word so that we may remain fruitful.

I encourage you to make a declaration as you pray, saying, "I am the branch. Jesus, you are the True Vine. I will abide in You. I am full of the Fruit of the Spirit. I am full of love, joy, peace, longsuffering, kindness, goodness, faithfulness, gentleness, and self-control. I will be fruitful in Jesus' name. Amen."

## 11. The Door

The Lord's sheep enter by the Door. That Door is Jesus as we learn about in John 10:7-9:

> Then Jesus said to them again, "Most assuredly, I say to you, I am the door of the sheep. All who ever came before Me are thieves and robbers, but the sheep did not hear them. I am the door. If anyone enters by Me, he will be saved, and will go in and out and find pasture."

A door is an opening for entering or leaving a house, tent, or room. In this passage, the Greek term for door is *thura*, which means 'portal, entrance, the opening', or 'the closure'. A door provides a way through as well as security, safety, and provision. Entering the sheepfold through Jesus is a saving action and provides us with abundant life and provision. We are safe and secure in Jesus Christ.

As the Door, faith in Jesus is the only way to enter the Kingdom of God. Furthermore, and as a result of the work on the cross, God extended to the Gentiles this same Door to salvation and the opportunity to know Him as Lord. Thus, Jesus is the Door for *all people, tribes, and nations* to enter into the abundant life as believers.

## 12. The Resurrection and the Life

In John 11:25, it says:

> *Jesus said to her, "I am the resurrection and the life. He who believes in Me, though he may die, he shall live."*

Resurrection is a doctrine, an event, and an act of persons being brought from death to unending life at the close of the age. As we read in the verse above, Jesus is the Resurrection of Life (the doctrine we live by). He pointed to the Resurrection of the righteous as resulting in eternal life (the act). Resurrection is also the final event that will usher Christians out of the bodily struggle of the present age into the glory which will accompany Jesus appearing in the clouds and blowing the trumpet.

Upon the Resurrection, we will have glorified bodies. They will be fit for our future life in Eternity. The power to bring this about is of God through Christ who has declared to us, *"I am the resurrection and the life."* Blessed are those who are resurrected in the name of the Lord!

Rest on the foundation of this Scripture. Be grounded in its truth and established in Him. He IS the Resurrection and the Life, now and forevermore!

Through the names of Jesus, we come to know who He is on a much deeper level. As such, we are enabled to approach Him in relationship and call on His name accordingly. This sweetens our fellowship with Him, elevates our prayers, and strengthens our faith walk. In addition, truly knowing the character of Jesus helps creates within us a pure heart of worship.

# CHAPTER FOUR

# Our Helper

The Holy Spirit is the third person of the Trinity or Godhead and the least known and understood. As our Helper, His contribution is most vital to our faith walk here on earth. He is intimately involved in our initial conversion and birth into the family of God. He is deeply invested in our ongoing development as Christians. He is the person through whom God acts, reveals His will, and empowers individuals in their Christian walk.

The Holy Spirit came to teach us, reinforcing what Jesus taught in order to bring us into right relationship with God. As part of that relationship, He desires to commune and fellowship with us in intimacy. Still, many do not know Him, neither do they know all about what He does in our lives and His purpose as part of our faith walk.

## The Person of the Holy Spirit

Many people do not think of the Holy Spirit as a real person—a spiritual being who is as real as the other members of the Trinity. As a result, they do not enjoy a relationship with Him.

It is of the highest importance from a practical standpoint that we get to know the Holy Spirit as a person. If we think of the Holy Spirit solely as an "it," an "influence," or a "power" (mystical or otherwise), our thoughts will likely be confined to, "How can I get more of the Holy Spirit?" Yet if we think of Him in the biblical way as a person, the Helper sent by God Himself, the Comforter that was sent to partner with us on our faith walk, our thoughts shift to include, "How can the Holy Spirit get more of me?"

The concept of the Holy Spirit being a mere "it," an "influence," or "power" inevitably leads to self-confidence, to self-exaltation, and to the exposure of self. How so? If the Holy Spirit is only an "it" that has some sort of influence and power to be drawn on at will, the tendency will be to rely more on self with the Holy Spirit's help being an afterthought. Furthermore, the transformative work He wants to do in and through a person is dismissed or thought to be irrelevant.

On the other hand, if we know the Holy Spirit as a real person, the knowledge of Him leads to love and humility. We love Him as a being of equal importance with the Father and the Son. At the same time, we recognize Him as being distinct in characteristics and personality apart from the Father and the Son yet still united to them in this mysterious oneness called the Trinity. We can accept His personhood within the Godhead, a member who is just as much a person as God the Father and God the Son.

In the same manner as we treat with reverence the Father and Son and what their distinct work has done for us and in us, we should have that same humble attitude towards the Holy Spirit and what He has to offer. Then, His transformative influence and power take on a whole new and much deeper meaning. As a result, we can surrender ourselves over to Him completely.

Let's take an even deeper look at the Holy Spirit...


## A Mighty Wind – Our Helper

The Spirit of God is often depicted as a mighty wind. One Greek word to describe the Spirit is *pnoé,* which means 'a blowing, wind, breath'. The mighty *pnoé* is described in Acts 2:1-2 which says:

> *When the Day of Pentecost had fully come, they were all with one accord in one place. And suddenly there came a sound from heaven, as of a rushing mighty wind, and it filled the whole house where they were sitting.*

In the Hebrew language, the word *ruach* for the Spirit of God is also used to describe Him. It means 'breath, wind, spirit'. In the Greek, another word often used is *pneuma*, and it is defined as 'wind, spirit'. There are abundant references to the wind of the Spirit of God found in both the Old and the New Testament. Let's take a look at a few of these references.

The Spirit exercised control over the chaotic waters at the beginning of creation. Genesis 1:2 says:

> *The earth was without form, and void; and darkness was on the face of the deep. And the Spirit of God was hovering over the face of the waters.*

As we read about in Exodus 14:21, God deployed this wind—the Spirit—to part the sea, thus enabling the Israelites to pass through safely and elude Pharaoh and his army.

> *Then Moses stretched out his hand over the sea; and the Lord caused the sea to go back by a strong east wind all that night, and made the sea into dry land, and the waters were divided.*

In the book of Matthew, chapter 3 verses 16-17 state:

> *When He had been baptized, Jesus came up immediately from the water; and behold, the heavens were opened to Him, and He saw the Spirit of God descending like a dove and alighting upon Him. And suddenly a voice came from heaven, saying, "This is My beloved Son, in whom I am well pleased."*

As we can see in this last passage, the Spirit was identified as a distinct member of the Trinity in this passage. Note that the descending of the Spirit like a dove and the Father's voice from Heaven showed that Jesus was another representation of God

Himself revealed in human form. This event also formed the connection between baptism and Christ's act of redemption.

The Spirit is also described as our Helper. In John 14:16-17, we read about Jesus' promise to send Him to us:

> *"And I will pray the Father, and He will give you another Helper, that He may abide with you forever—the Spirit of truth, whom the world cannot receive, because it neither sees Him nor knows Him; but you know Him, for He dwells with you and will be in you."*

Then in John 14:26, Jesus tells us:

> *"But the Helper, the Holy Spirit, whom the Father will send in My name, He will teach you all things, and bring to your remembrance all things that I said to you."*

Later in John 15:26, Jesus says:

> *"But when the Helper comes, whom I shall send to you from the Father, the Spirit of truth who proceeds from the Father, He will testify of Me."*

As you have read, Jesus made these promises that the Holy Spirit would come, calling Him our Helper. The Greek word for helper is *paraklétos*. It is derived from *pará*, which means 'close beside', and *kaléo* meaning 'make a call'. Hence, as the Helper, the Holy Spirit has been called to be close by our side. The significance of this word means that the Holy Spirit is called to be our Comforter, our Intercessor, our Advocate, our Counselor, our Strengthener, and our Standby.

In non-biblical literature, *paraklétos* has a technical meaning of 'an attorney who appears in court on behalf of another'. In a similar manner, the Holy Spirit is always there to guide us, lead us to the truth, to help us in times of trouble, to defend us, to speak on our behalf, and to strengthen us to be able to endure this world's system. He is the best Advocate that we can have!

The word 'spirit' is occasionally interchanged with the word 'ghost', meaning 'most holy one or thing'. This is why you will sometimes hear the Holy Spirit referred to as the Holy Ghost. In essence, this is simply another name for Him as well as a facet of His being.

Our Helper is the ultimate origin of all mental and spiritual gifts. Not only did biblical prophets benefit from the influence of the Spirit, but the Spirit will be poured out upon all the people of God as we read about in Joel 2:28.

> *"And it shall come to pass afterward that I will pour out My Spirit on all flesh; Your sons and your daughters shall prophesy, your old men shall dream dreams, your young men shall see visions."*

Our reception of the Spirit is dependent upon repentance and is associated with the creation of a new heart. Once we have confessed our sins and accepted the Lord Jesus as our Savior, we have full access to the Spirit and what He has to offer. We must choose to receive Him.

We are living in an hour where we need the Holy Spirit now more than ever. If we are to experience a spiritual awakening and revival in the land, we will need the mighty wind of the Spirit to blow. If we are to upgrade our worship and not walk in strange fire, we will need the Helper to be close beside us.

The hour has come for every minister and every church body to come face-to-face with the Holy Spirit. Sadly, there are denominations that have not accepted the Holy Spirit and His work, including the manifestations of miracles. Whether we believe in Him or not, the Holy Spirit is going to continue and complete His assignment here on earth. Only those who have their spiritual eyes and ears open to see and hear will perceive the importance of cultivating a close relationship with the Holy Spirit and living the Spirit-led life.

## The Personality of the Holy Spirit

The Holy Spirit has a personality—a mind, a will, and emotions. As such, He can be grieved, quenched, blasphemed, and lied to.

## 1. The Holy Spirit can be grieved.

In Ephesians 4:30, it says:

*And do not grieve the Holy Spirit of God, by whom you were sealed for the day of redemption.*

You may ask, "How exactly can I grieve the Holy Spirit?"

In response, my question to you is, "Does it grieve you when someone does not take you at your word, thinks you're lying, and calls you a liar? What about if someone dismisses you as irrelevant or treats you as if you don't matter?"

Not being taken at our word and having people think and tell us we are lying can be very upsetting. If who we are and what we offer is treated as if it was nothing, this is extremely hurtful. It *grieves* us.

Well, the Holy Spirit tells us things through the Word of God as well as impresses us with truth deep in our spirits. He has come to be our Helper in all areas. If we do not believe Him, it causes Him grief. If we resist His help, it deeply saddens Him.

Here's another scenario and question for you... Imagine a parent who has tried their best to steer their child into the path of right living where they are responsible and make good decisions. Yet, that child rebels and insists on doing things their own way, and they are led down destructive paths. Do you not think that parent would be heartbroken?

In the same manner, when we give our word and fail to fulfill that word, it grieves the Holy Spirit. When we do something unholy when the Holy Spirit is living inside us ready to help us make better choices, it causes Him grief. Every time we rebel in any way, He is heartbroken.

## 2. The Holy Spirit can be quenched.

1 Thessalonians 5:19 states:

*Do not quench the Spirit.*

Quench means 'extinguish, cool suddenly, or put out'. In other words, it means that, in the case of the Holy Spirit, His influence is being put out, ignored, tamped down, dismissed, and set aside.

How does this happen? It's called distraction! The way to quench the Spirit is by doing things and having attitudes that have the same effect as throwing a bucket of water on a fire. They distract us from the person and work of the Holy Spirit, leading us to dismissing His help and guidance in our lives.

Here are a few examples...

I have noticed in our churches that, as the service starts, the same people come to church late every Sunday. When they make their grand entrance, all eyes turn to them, and they effectively disrupt the worship. Another example is when, after the Pastor has completed the message and an altar call to receive Jesus has been given, members of the congregation noisily begin to exit the building. That's a distraction to the person deciding to give their lives to Christ. It is disrespectful.

What about examples in our everyday lives? When we ignore that "still small voice" inside of us that causes us to pause and think about a decision, acting as a "check" in the spirit, we quench the Spirit's voice. When we get caught up in doing our own thing in our own strength without checking in with Him about how we need to handle a situation or what direction we need to go, that pushes Him aside and extinguishes His influence and God's leading.

### 3. The Holy Spirit can be blasphemed.

Blaspheming of the Spirit is found in Mark 3:29:

*"but he who blasphemes against the Holy Spirit never has forgiveness, but is subject to eternal condemnation."* —

Blasphemy is to deny, renounce, or reject the Holy Spirit's testimony concerning Jesus as Savior and Lord. In other words, if the Holy Spirit witnesses to a person's spirit that Jesus Christ is Savior and Lord, and that person rejects Him in unbelief and refuses to accept Him as Lord, that person cannot be forgiven. They have rejected the only way to be forgiven.

Peter says in Acts 4:12:

*"Nor is there salvation in any other, for there is no other name under heaven given among men by which we must be saved."*

Jesus Christ is the *only way* to the Father. Rejecting the only way of salvation is unforgiveable and leads to eternal death.

### 4. The Holy Spirit can be lied to.

In Acts 5:1-4, we read:

*But a certain man named Ananias, with Sapphira his wife, sold a possession. And he kept back part of the proceeds, his wife also being aware of it, and brought a certain part and laid it at the apostles' feet. But Peter said, "Ananias, why has Satan filled your heart to lie to the Holy Spirit and keep back part of the price of the land for yourself? While it remained, was it not your own? And after it was sold, was it not in your own control? Why have you conceived this thing in your heart? You have not lied to men but to God."*

Ananias and Sapphira lied to the Holy Spirit. If you read further in the story, you find out that lying to the Spirit had very serious consequences in the end for this couple. This story also illustrates the equality that God the Father and God the Son have with God the Holy Spirit. If you lie to one, you've lied to all the Godhead.

## The Holy Spirit's Duties

There are many duties that the Holy Spirit has regarding His interaction with believers. They all come under the mantle of being our Helper as Jesus promised.

**1. He baptizes us.**

The Greek word for baptize is *baptizo*, which means 'to immerse or submerge'. Therefore, when one is baptized, they are fully immersed—encompassed and enveloped—by whatever they are being baptized into.

The Holy Spirit is the Baptizer. His duty is to baptize believers into the Body of Christ for the purpose of salvation. As 1 Corinthians 12:13 states:

> *For by one Spirit we were all baptized into one body—whether Jews or Greeks, whether slaves or free—and have all been made to drink into one Spirit.*

Once an individual surrenders their life to Jesus, the believer is baptized *by* the Holy Spirit. The element into which the believer is baptized is the Body of Christ. Note that this is not water baptism.

the wall that separated us from Him has been broken down by Jesus Christ, the Anointed One, and what He did for us. We are enabled to walk in His favor and provision. The whole Christian life—our relationship and access to the Most High—is the result of God's grace in which we stand.

John 16:14 says:

*He will glorify Me, for He will take of what is Mine and declare it to you.*

The Holy Spirit's ministry is not only directed to believers but also to Christ. What the Spirit teaches, He draws from and conveys in the authority of Christ. He declares and reveals to us everything that comes from the Father, that which has been given to our Savior, giving us full access to what God has for us. This glorifies Christ.

In the same manner, when we are in true ministry as unto the Lord, we cannot operate according to our own private agenda. Instead, we answer to a higher authority and must glorify God in all that we do.

### 3. He teaches us and brings all things to our remembrance.

The Holy Spirit's ministry is predominantly Christ-oriented, teaching and reminding us of the teachings of Jesus and the Word. The Spirit is not self-serving.

We read about this in John 14:26:

> *But the Helper, the Holy Spirit, whom the Father will send in My name, He will teach you all things, and bring to your remembrance all things that I said to you.*

Our Helper is our tutor in all things related to God and godliness. In reinforcing the teachings of Jesus, He encourages us in our faith walk, helping us through life and ministry so that we are strengthened for every good work.

### 4. He gives us wisdom and revelation.

Ephesians 1:17 says:

> *that the God of our Lord Jesus Christ, the Father of glory, may give to you the spirit of wisdom and revelation in the knowledge of Him,*

The real essence of wisdom is spiritual. Wisdom is a spirit that only God can give. This wisdom is a demonstration of practical and workable principles, solutions, and applications. Revelation refers to clear perception and applicable understanding given regarding things previously unknown. The Holy Spirit is the divine source of both wisdom and revelation.

## 5. He intercedes for us.

Intercession is the action of praying for or intervening on behalf of another person. As our Advocate, the Holy Spirit intercedes for us according to the will of God. As Romans 8:26-27 says:

*Likewise the Spirit also helps in our weaknesses. For we do not know what we should pray for as we ought, but the Spirit Himself makes intercession for us with groanings which cannot be uttered. Now He who searches the hearts knows what the mind of the Spirit is, because He makes intercession for the saints according to the will of God.*

God knows and searches our hearts. He understands all the imaginations and the thoughts we have and are struggling with. He is not unaware of our weaknesses and where we need His assistance.

Therefore, we have been given the Holy Spirit who intercedes for us on our behalf. This means He stands in the gap for us. He helps us in our weaknesses. When we do not know what to pray, He prays for us and gives us the words.

## 6. He strengthens the inner man.

God's intention is that we become mighty in power.

In Ephesians 3:16, we read:

> that He would grant you, according to the riches of His
> glory, to be strengthened with might through His Spirit in
> the inner man,

The Holy Spirit empowers believers on the inside. He empowers them for the work of the ministry. His desire is for us to be tenacious, strong, and to manifest staying power. He wants us to have an inner strength to withstand tough times and to verbalize our trust in Him. We cannot succeed in our own strength, power, and might, but it is only *"by My Spirit"* (Zechariah 4:6) that we are empowered for the work God has for us.

## 7. He endows the believer with spiritual gifts.

In 1 Corinthians 12:1-11, we read about spiritual gifts. They are given to each of us for the profit of all. (v. 7) These diverse and different gifts are distributed by the Spirit. Verse 11 tells us:

> But one and the same Spirit works all these things,
> distributing to each one individually as He wills.

Spiritual gifts are another one of God's promises. God gives skills and abilities through His Spirit to all Christians to equip them to serve Him as He wills. These gifts were placed in the Church as resources to be utilized at the point of need for ministry by the Body of Christ. They come together in unity through each member of the Body exercising their gift to the glory of God.

Do you know what your gift(s) are? If not, ask God to reveal it/them to you by the Spirit.

## The Holy Spirit is The Deity.

The Holy Spirit is not only a person, He is a deity. A deity is a being who is divine—a god. The Holy Spirit is not just any god, He is The Deity, a member of the Trinity or Godhead.

In Psalms 139:7-10, we see this characteristic of the Holy Spirit revealed:

> Where can I go from Your Spirit? Or where can I flee from Your presence? If I ascend into heaven, You are there; If I make my bed in hell, behold, You are there. If I take the wings of the morning, and dwell in the uttermost parts of the sea, even there Your hand shall lead me, and Your right hand shall hold me.

As part of the Holy Trinity, the Holy Spirit is everywhere. Another word for this is omnipresent, which is an attribute of God alone. It means that God is free from the laws or limitations of space. God's presence is felt in all parts of the universe. No one can escape His presence. His presence is not governed by bodily contact but revealed through knowledge and relationship.

# Be Filled with the Spirit

Speaking to the Ephesian Christians, Paul exhorted them in Ephesians 5:18 to *"be filled with the Spirit"*. Being filled with the Holy Spirit is for every believer. It is not a once-and-for-all experience, but it is an indwelling that He intends to have repeated time and time again. It means to be filled and to keep being filled.

The filling of the Spirit involves being given power and boldness for God's service. Being constantly filled with the Spirit is not a matter of receiving more of Him, but it is about opening more of ourselves to Him in order to have a stronger relationship each and every day. It is a matter of desiring Him to fully occupy, guide, and control every area of our lives. It is meant to provide strength to meet any crisis or challenge encountered in everyday living. Then, whatever life brings, His power is made more evident in and through us.

Through the indwelling of the Spirit, we are delivered from the power of sin when we first come to know Christ. Then, it is by the Holy Spirit's power that we live and grow in Christ in our daily walk of faith. When this happens, the Fruit of the Spirit begins to manifest in our lives. For example, His joy and peace control our emotions. Our inner thoughts and motives are guided by Him. Essentially, when we are filled with the Holy Spirit, we become subject to His control.

If you do not know the Holy Spirit personally...

- Are you ready to meet Him?
- Do you want to know Him as a person?
- Do you want to hear His voice?

The Holy Spirit is waiting for you to come and meet Him! He longs to fill your life with all power and authority that comes with this indwelling, this personal relationship with Him.

I personally have experienced who the Holy Spirit is in my life. He is gentle, beautiful, most precious, and loving. I make it a habit to say, "Good morning, Holy Spirit" each day. His presence makes me feel incredibly loved, accepted, and wanted, so much so that my heart bubbles over with joy. He has shown Himself to be mighty as well as gentle. When He comes upon me, every fiber of my being feels His power.

You can experience the Holy Spirit like this as well! Like I said, He is waiting for you, ready to meet you and get intimately acquainted.

God has made us to be vessels of His Holy Spirit. His purpose for us is found in Ephesians 3:19b: *"...that ye might be filled with all the fullness of God."* (KJV) Therefore, we must empty ourselves of our own selfish cares and desires so that the fullness of God—His Spirit—can come in.

It is time to ask yourself... "Have I given myself wholly and without reservation to God and to His Spirit?" If you have not, are you willing to pray this prayer of surrender? If so, please join me in praying the following prayer:

"Lord Jesus, I lay it all down at the foot of the cross. I surrender my spirit, soul, and body to You. I give You my weaknesses, my sins, my fears, and my failure as well as my hopes and dreams. Please take this helpless, corrupt, frail body of mine and make it a vessel fit for Your use. I invite the Holy Spirit in to fill me now and every day for the rest of my life. In Jesus' name and by Your Spirit. Amen!"

If you prayed this prayer, know that He *will* answer you. He *will* pour out His Spirit upon your life. He *will* fill you with unspeakable joy. He will do all this and more, for He promises in John 14:14, *"If you ask anything in My name, I will do it."*

## Speaking in Tongues

Now that we know that being filled with the Holy Spirit is for every believer, what is one of the manifestations that is available to us once we have been filled with the Holy Spirit?

Let's read about it in Act 2:1-4:

> *When the Day of Pentecost had fully come, they were all with one accord in one place. And suddenly there came a sound from heaven, as of a rushing mighty wind, and it filled the whole house where they were sitting. Then there appeared to them divided tongues, as of fire, and one sat upon each of them. And they were all filled with the Holy Spirit and began to speak with other tongues, as the Spirit gave them utterance.*

The Day of Pentecost was the coming of the Holy Spirit that Jesus promised would be sent after He ascended to Heaven. Now, notice that they were ALL filled with the Holy Spirit at Pentecost, all 120 of them who were waiting in the upper room. (Acts 1:12-15, 2:4) The second phenomenal thing that happened is documented in verse 4: *"And they all were filled with the Holy Spirit __and__ began to speak with other tongues."*[1] Please note the subject of the sentence is THEY. The "they" who were all filled with the Holy Spirit is the same "they" who began to speak with other tongues. In other words, the 120 were *first* filled with the Holy Spirit, *and then*, they all spoke as the Spirit gave them utterance.

There has been much controversy over the years concerning this Scripture, especially with regard to *"other tongues."* As a result of a lack of understanding, many in the Church haven't

---

[1] Emphasis mine

experienced the fullness of being filled with the Holy Spirit through the ability of speaking in tongues.

It is obvious these people at Pentecost spoke in tongues other than their native language. The word 'tongues' in the Greek is the word *glosse.* It actually means 'languages', for it is the plural form of the word *'glossa'.* Thus, speaking in tongues by the Holy Spirit involves many tongues and languages other than your own native language.

One of the things we need to understand about tongues is that it serves a vital purpose and has significant benefits in the life of the believer. Part of the misunderstanding surrounding tongues is fueled by fear and confusion over this manifestation of being filled by the Spirit. If we truly comprehend the purpose and benefits behind speaking in tongues, it brings understanding.

1. **Tongues edify the speaker.**

Scripture says in 1 Corinthians 14:4a:

*He who speaks in a tongue edifies himself….*

Edify means 'to build up'. When you pray in an unknown tongue, it builds up your inner person. Thus, the human spirit is made stronger through the use of tongues.

## 2. Tongues are spoken to God.

1 Corinthians 14:2a (NIV) tells us this:

> For anyone who speaks in a tongue does not speak to people but to God...

Tongues are a form of communion with God—spirit to Spirit. Because it is inspired by the Holy Spirit and not of our own utterance, it is a pure form of prayer since our "self" (mind, will, and emotions) is out of the way. It is your spirit that is praying as we read about in 1 Corinthians 14:14.

## 3. Mysteries are spoken in tongues.

When we look at the second half of 1 Corinthians 14:2 (NIV), we read:

> Indeed, no one understands them; they utter mysteries by the Spirit.

This prayer language speaks of secret truths and hidden things not obvious to our human understanding. These mysteries become powerful prayers that work on our behalf. They also open our spirits to receive the mysteries of God and bring revelation that we cannot attain by ourselves.

### 4. Tongues aid us in our prayers.

Remember the Scripture from Romans 8:26 that we discussed earlier? Let's read it from the NLV this time:

*...We do not know how to pray or what we should pray for, but the Holy Spirit prays to God for us with sounds that cannot be put into words.*

When we are weak or struggling with how to pray and what to pray, switching to tongues aligns our prayers to God's will. Through tongues, the Holy Spirit does the praying for us.

### 5. Tongues help us express what is in our spirit.

As believers, we are designed to commune with God in prayer, petitions, thanksgiving, praise, and worship. Sometimes, mere words cannot express what is deep inside our spirits. Tongues is one way of letting our spirits express ourselves to God in a deeper way.

Tongues are a great, personal blessing to the believer. As discussed, the purpose of tongues comes with distinct benefits that will bless every Christian who seeks this gift as part of being filled with the Holy Spirit.

In seeking an intimate relationship with the Holy Spirit, we tap into who He is, what He has to offer, and access the power of His indwelling, including speaking in tongues. This requires us to give more of ourselves to Him in the way of surrender, giving Him all the control over every aspect of our lives. As our Helper, we can trust Him!

# CHAPTER FIVE

## Renewed In Knowledge

The Body of Christ has suffered unnecessary pain, confusion, disbelief, and other struggles due to the lack of knowledge of who God really is. These struggles are considered struggles with the flesh. Those who belong to Christ are to crucify the flesh with its passions and desires. (Galatians 5:24)

Paul puts it another way. He says in Romans 8:13 (KJV) that we are to mortify the flesh. Mortify in the Greek means 'to kill', 'become dead', or 'put to death'. What this means is that we must make a choice to live by the Spirit by putting to death fleshly mindsets, attitudes, and actions. We are to leave the sinful nature behind—it was crucified with Christ—and walk in the knowledge of who we are now because of Him.

1 Peter 2:11 (NLT) states:

> Dear friends, I warn you as "temporary residents and foreigners" to keep away from worldly desires that wage war against your very souls.

The flesh wars against our very souls. This is something we must deal with daily. In fact, resisting the flesh is a command, for not doing so leads to death.

# Renewed and Transformed

No preacher can lay hands on you and make your fleshly struggles suddenly disappear. In the Scripture you just read, Peter tells us that it is *our* job to keep away from things of the flesh. In the NKJV, the word that is used is 'abstain'. In the Greek, this word is a verb or action that means 'to hold back, keep off, to be away, be distant'. In other words, it means to intentionally restrain yourself from doing or enjoying something. It also means to keep your hands off, deny yourself, avoid the situation, and let it alone. When it comes to dealing with the flesh, we have to deliberately ACT in a way that repels and denies the old nature and puts on our new nature in Christ.

As Colossians 3:10 (NLT) states it:

*Put on your new nature, and be renewed as you learn to know your Creator and become like him.*

The AMP Bible puts it this way:

*and have put on the new [spiritual] self who is being continually renewed in true knowledge in the image of Him who created the new self—*

Please read this Scripture again slowly. Let it integrate deep into your spirit. Our ability to reflect our new nature is found as we renew ourselves in the true knowledge of our God. We must come to know Him!

Notice that the AMP version also talks of this being a continuous thing. Knowing God requires our constant investment in the relationship. Being renewed daily is a commitment necessary for us to become like Jesus, reflecting His image. The AMPC puts it as our spiritual self being *"[ever in the process of being] renewed and remolded"*. We are ALL a work in progress.

Furthermore, it is TIME that we start making some progress on this important issue of being renewed in the knowledge of our Lord. It is a foundational piece for our faith walk. Why? Because time is of the essence, for Jesus is on His way back!

- What will He find in us when He returns?
- Will He find a church that is made new and transformed? *OR...*
- Will He find us caught in the snares of an old nature even though He already provided the way for us to be rid of it for good?

Matthew 12:35-37 tells us that:

*"A good man out of the good treasure of his heart brings forth good things, and an evil man out of the evil treasure brings forth evil things. But I say to you that for every idle word men may speak, they will give account of it in the day of judgment. For by your words you will be justified, and by your words you will be condemned."*

If any negative qualities are in us, we put them there or allowed them to take root. This may or may not have been intentional, but if we have entertained negative thoughts or held on to ungodly mindsets or let sinful desires and tendencies germinate in our hearts, these things (evil treasure) will eventually come forth. Instead, we are to fill our hearts with that which is pure and holy (good treasure).

We learn more about this in Ephesians 4:22-24 where Paul exhorts us to:

> ...put off, concerning your former conduct, the old man which grows corrupt according to the deceitful lusts, and be renewed in the spirit of your mind, and that you put on the new man which was created according to God, in true righteous-ness and holiness.

In this Scripture, we clearly see the contrast between a lifestyle dominated by disobedience and a lifestyle governed by obedience with the help of the Holy Spirit's power. The command to put off the old man or nature is what happens at salvation, but it is also the abstaining that is required of us as believers as discussed at the beginning of this chapter.

What are some of the things that we are to put off? We are to put away lying, wrath, acting in anger, stealing, bitterness and resentment, malice and evil intent, corrupt and unwholesome speech, quarrelling, and anything else that gives a foothold for the devil to work in our lives. These things grieve the Holy Spirit. (Ephesians 4:25-32)

As believers, we must choose to leave the old way of being and behaving behind and live a renewed life that reflects who Jesus is. We are to be transformed.

2 Corinthians 3:18 (AMP) says:

*And we all, with unveiled face, continually seeing as in a mirror the glory of the Lord, are progressively being transformed into His image from [one degree of] glory to [even more] glory, which comes from the Lord, [who is] the Spirit.*

Pause. Let this soak in! Again, this verse reminds us that we are a work in progress...but that progress must indeed be made. It is the only way we can be transformed into the image of Christ.

What is that image? The Bible calls it the glory of God. As we continually look to Jesus (as if gazing into a mirror), we see Him become our reflection. We are transformed into the glory. The more we look to Him, the more we become renewed in knowledge according to the image of Him that created us. It is all done by the Spirit of the Lord. This is how we move from glory to glory.

# Meditation

One of the tools that we can employ to be renewed in the knowledge of our Lord is the use of meditation. Meditation means 'to reflect, to moan, to mutter, to ponder'. The sum of what meditation involves in this context is first reading the Word, declaring it, walking in it, and allowing it to guide you. Through meditation, we spend TIME with the Word where we reflect on it deeply and pray for Holy Spirit to reveal all that He desires for us to receive.

As part of meditation, personalizing and memorizing Scripture is another strategy. As each Scripture is personalized and memorized, we allow it to sink deep within our hearts and spirits, letting it transform us from the inside out. In addition, we are to visualize it in our mind's eye as already accomplished or true in our lives. Seeing things as accomplished and a reality not only strengthens our faith, but it is the essence of faith.

Take a look at what Hebrews 11:1 (TLB) says:

*What is faith? It is the confident assurance that something we want is going to happen. It is the certainty that what we hope for is waiting for us, even though we cannot see it up ahead.*

When we align our wants and hopes to what is found in the Word, we have the assurance that God will fulfill it. As we meditate on Scripture and hide it deep in our hearts, it transforms us. This sets us up to receive and be successful because our thoughts and desires are renewed to line up with the Father's will.

Joshua 1:8 says:

*This Book of the Law shall not depart from your mouth, but you shall meditate in it day and night, that you may observe to do according to all that is written in it. For then you will make your way prosperous, and then you will have good success.*

Therefore, simply knowing God's Word is not enough. Any one of us may be able to recite the Word from memory, but if it hasn't permeated down into our hearts, it will not help us in the situations we find ourselves in. As such, memorizing for memorization's sake is not sufficient. It must be paired with meditation that leads to deep learning and transformation.

In Psalms 1:2, we read:

*But his delight is in the law of the Lord, and in His law he meditates day and night.*

As we meditate in the Word, something actually happens within our spirits. There is a heavenly knowledge transfer into us that we may not immediately be aware of. As a result, we are changed by what we read.

How can this be so? Let's look at a practical example of how this works...

What if we constantly listened to negative reports on the news and read about violence and crimes being committed. While most of us don't become what we see, hear, or read, something still happens inside of us. For one, we become much more fearful. Why? Because we are spirit beings. Our spirit is molded and fed by words and what we take in through what we see and are exposed to. Eventually, what we absorb will affect us in one way or another.

On the other hand, when we behold the Word of God in Spirit, it has the power to change us for our good and His glory. The more we look to God through the Word—read it, listen to it, meditate on it, and soak it all in—the more we become transfigured. The knowledge of the Word and the promises and life that it contains becomes our reality, causing us to rise above any situation or circumstance.

## Be a Doer of the Word

Many people have the mistaken idea that hearing a good sermon or Bible study is what causes them to grow and receive God's blessing. However, it is not the hearing but the *doing* that brings blessing. Sadly, too many Christians mark their Bibles and take notes, but the Word is not embedded in their hearts. They fail to put into practice that which they have been taught.

James 1:22-25 says:

*But be doers of the word, and not hearers only, deceiving yourselves. For if anyone is a hearer of the word and not a doer, he is like a man observing his natural face in a mirror; for he observes himself, goes away, and immediately forgets what kind of man he was. But he who looks into the perfect law of liberty and continues in it, and is not a forgetful hearer but a doer of the work, this one will be blessed in what he does.*

In verse 22, we receive the very specific command from God to be a DOER of the Word. It is not enough just to hear it and then dismiss it. It is not enough to read it and do nothing with it. It is not enough to pay attention during a Sunday morning sermon or Bible study night but then promptly forget it. No, we must *act* on what we have read and let the Word do its work in us.

Let's meditate on the analogy from this passage a bit more...

When one looks in a mirror, they are able to see all the blemishes and imperfections in their reflection. Naturally, they are moved by what they see. As long as the imperfections, spots, and ugliness remain up close and personal, it is easy to do something about them. But when they walk away from the mirror, those blemishes and defects are easily forgotten, and they are no longer bothered by them. As a result, nothing changes.

So it is with the Word. As long as we study it—looking into it as a mirror—we are able to see within ourselves those things that need to be transformed to be more like Jesus. We are inspired and motivated to constantly seek to improve ourselves and conform to the teaching of the Word. We become willing to give way to the Holy Spirit so that He can perform a makeover.

The following are common mistakes people make when they "look into the mirror" spiritually:

### 1. They merely glance at themselves.

They do not carefully examine themselves and their hearts as they read the Word. Many sincere believers read a chapter of the Bible each day, but it is only a religious exercise. They fail to profit from it personally. A superficial reading of the Bible will never reveal our deepest needs and lead to the transformative work that the Lord wants to do to make us like Him.

### 2. They forget what they see.

If they looked deeply enough into their hearts, what they would see would be unforgettable! Think of how some individuals in the Bible responded to the true knowledge of their own hearts. Isaiah cried, *"Woe is me! For I am undone!"* (Isaiah 6:5) Peter cried, *"Depart from me, for I am a sinful man, O Lord!"* (Luke 5:8) Coming to the end of themselves where they recognized their great need allowed the Lord to do His mighty work in them.

### 3. They fail to obey what the Word tells them to do.

They think that hearing is the same as doing...and it is not. If we are to use God's mirror properly, then we must gaze into it carefully and with serious intent. No quick glances will do. We must examine our own hearts and lives in the light of God's Word. Then, we must implement what God is saying to us, allowing His Spirit to change us through our acts of obedience. That is being a doer.

This requires our time, attention, and sincere devotion. Five minutes with God each day will never accomplish a deep spiritual examination. We must dedicate ourselves to the study of the Word, to meditation, and spending time in the presence of God, for it is only through this intimate relationship with Him that we can be truly renewed in knowledge.

It is God's desire that we all come to the knowledge of Him who is the Truth and the Life for all who believe.

1 Timothy 2:3-4 states:

> *For this is good and acceptable in the sight of God our Savior, who desires all men to be saved and to come to the knowledge of the truth.*

The word knowledge in this text means 'to know, recognize, become fully acquainted with, acknowledge, perceive', and 'have knowledge and full discernment'. This is a "knowing" that is deep, profound, and life changing.

What does this mean for you?

There should be a "knowing" in you that Jesus Christ is the Son of the living God. There should be a "knowing" in you that He died, was buried, and rose again on the third day. There should be a "knowing" in you that you can walk in freedom because of Jesus' death and resurrection. There should be a "knowing" in you that you can stand boldly on the Word in spite of everything that is happening in the natural realm. There should be a "knowing" in you that God is for you and not against you. In other words, you should have this confident inner recognition that comes with being intimately acquainted with your Lord and Savior.

So, as you continue to walk in renewed knowledge, remember what you have learned. Renewed in knowledge means a transformed life. It is a work in progress that requires you to put off those things that are related to the flesh and an old nature. To be truly transformed, it is imperative that you meditate on the Word, letting it permeate your spirit and overtake you. Finally, you must become a doer of Word, putting action to what you are hearing and reading. This is the life of a believer who is moving from glory to glory by the Spirit.

# CHAPTER SIX

# The Power of Prayer

Prayer is probably one of the most talked about and discussed topic in the Church. Yet, it appears to be the least used power that is available to the Body of Christ. This is evidenced by the fact that there are way too many believers who struggle in the area of prayer.

Why is this so?

Perhaps people don't know how to pray or pray effectively. Some Christians may have become so discouraged because they feel like prayer is a fruitless ritual with little to no evidence of tangible results. Maybe their time spent in prayer has produced little in the way of results, leading them to conclude, even subconsciously, that they would rather try and figure things out on their own. Many more have simply quit the practice and avoided any opportunity to participate in it for one reason or another. The point is that many people are disillusioned about prayer.

If we wish to be truly honest, more among us than not are suffering from a silent disillusionment with our experience with prayer. We have asked ourselves questions like:

- "Does it really work?"

- "Do my prayers make a difference?"

- "Can it truly change my circumstances?"

- "Am I just wasting my time?"

- "What's the point?"

- "Is He even listening?"

If you have harbored any of these same questions or others like it with regard to prayer, it is time to learn more about what prayer is really all about. It is time to dispel the disillusionment so that you can see the power prayer has and be empowered to wield this weapon effectively.

Despite questions, confusion, and uncertainty surrounding prayer, it is still the greatest common denominator among all the great biblical characters and millions of believers throughout history. Some of these prayer giants include Abraham, Moses, Joseph, David, Solomon, Esther, Deborah, Daniel, and Paul just to name a few. They each had a dynamic and profound commitment to prayer. Their records show the direct impact of prayer in their lives and their effect on the circumstances and situations they faced. This evidence affirms that one thing is sure...no matter what you may think about prayer, *it works!*

# What is prayer?

To start off with, prayer is a spiritual discipline that the Lord has commanded His people to partake in. With that said, let's explore some key aspects of what prayer is.

## 1. Prayer is communicating with God.

Through prayer, we communicate and have fellowship with God. It is having a conversation with the Most High. It is through prayer that we have continuous access to the One who created us. Thus, it leads us into His presence. As a result, prayer is key to building our relationship with the Godhead.

## 2. Prayer is an avenue that ushers in the presence of God.

Here are a couple of examples as found in Scripture:

At the transfiguration of Christ, we learn that *"As he was praying, the appearance of his face changed, and his clothes became as bright as a flash of lightning."* (Luke 9:29, NIV) The very presence of God came down and illuminated Jesus as he was praying.

On the Day of Pentecost when the Holy Spirit came down on those waiting in the upper room, we know from Scripture in Acts 1:14 (NIV) that they had *"all joined together constantly in prayer"*. It was prayer that preceded the outpouring of the Holy Spirit's presence.

3. **Prayer is giving God and Heaven the legal right and permission to get involved in earth's affairs.**

God has granted each and every one of us free will. This means that we get to choose for ourselves. Thus, He will never force us to do anything, including involving Him in our affairs. With that said, He waits for our invitation through prayer to get involved in our lives and in the world around us. Once He has permission, He is released to do His best work.

4. **Prayer is exercising our legal authority as a co-heir with Christ to invoke Heaven's influence on the planet.**

Because of the work of the cross, we have been made co-heirs with Christ. He gave us all authority to do the work of the Father here on earth. We have been given the legal right to bring down to earth that which has already been declared and decreed in Heaven. In other words, our prayers come into agreement with His will and serve a critical role in seeing all Heaven move on our behalf.

5. **Prayer is presenting our requests to God.**

As we learn in Philippians 4:6, we are to present our requests to God through prayer. Other words to describe this form of prayer is 'petition', 'supplication', or 'entreaty'. This is where we share with God and lay at His feet our specific requests and needs. It is where we acknowledge our need for Him and His help. We have the conversation, we invite Him in and give Him permission to work, and we agree that His will be done.

## Coming into Agreement with God

It is important that our prayers come into agreement with God and what He wants to do—His will. He has the big picture in mind, and He sees things that we do not. Also, His thoughts are not our thoughts. (Isaiah 55:8) Our obedience in aligning ourselves to His will in our prayer life results in mighty things happening in our lives and in the world around us.

We cannot come into agreement with God if we do not know Him. Like we talked about in the last chapter, we must be renewed in the knowledge of Him, and that is done, in part, through our study of the Word. Having conversations with God—our prayer life—is another requirement that builds that relationship so that we can step out in agreement with God and what He wants to do.

As part of our conversations with God, He speaks to us. Occasionally, this may happen in an audible voice, but mostly, it is within our own spirits that we hear His voice in return. Without a prayer life, we aren't as tuned into His voice and what He has to say.

God does not need anything in the sense that He is lacking anything, for He is God and lacks nothing. However, His desire ("need") is for His people to agree with Him through their prayers so that He can accomplish His work here on earth more effectively. This is one of the primary purposes for our walk with God on this side of Heaven.

Here are some examples from the Word:

- To rescue humanity and living creatures from the Flood, God needed Noah. (Genesis 6:9-22)

- For the creation of a great nation, God needed Abraham. (Genesis 12:1-3)

- To lead the nation of Israel, God needed Moses. (Exodus 3:7-10)

- To defeat Jericho, God needed Joshua. (Joshua 6)

- For the preservation of the Hebrews, God needed Esther. (Esther 4 and 7)

- For the salvation of mankind, God needed to become man (Jesus). (Isaiah 53)

Each of these individuals had a relationship with God. They talked to Him in prayer, and they heard back from Him on what they must do. They submitted to what He asked of them, and this agreement brought about some incredible results.

# Why should we pray?

There are many reasons why we should pray. We have already learned about some of those reasons as were shared earlier:

- It is a way to communicate with God.

- It ushers in the presence of God.

- It gives God permission to work in our lives.

- It exercises our legal authority as given to us by Christ.

- It allows us to present our requests and needs to God.

- It is a way to come into agreement with God and His purposes.

Like we have also learned, prayer fosters a relationship with God and teaches us to tune into His voice. However, there are other important reasons why we are to engage in prayer.

## 1. God commands us to pray.

In Luke 18:1 (NIV), we read:

*Then Jesus told his disciples a parable to show them that they should always pray and not give up.*

1 Chronicles 16:11 (NIV) says:

*Look to the Lord and His strength; seek his face always.*

We must seek the Lord (pray) always. Plus, we are not to give up in our prayers. This is a lifelong commitment in our relationship with God.

## 2. We are to involve God in everything that we do.

Involving God in everything that we do is also a commandment of the Lord. As we read in Psalms 37:5 (NLT):

> *Commit everything you do to the Lord. Trust him, and he will help you.*

Unfortunately, some people treat God like they do a lawyer. They only go to Him when they are in trouble or desperate. Instead, we are to submit our prayers, supplications, and petitions to God on every occasion and not just when we are in trouble or in a desperate state. The Word says in Philippians 4:6 that we are to literally *"pray about everything."* (NLT)

## 3. Prayer is foundational for success.

He who ceases to pray ceases to prosper. That's right! Our success is dependent on our prayer life.

Proverbs 16:3 (AMP) states:

> *Commit your works to the Lord [submit and trust them to Him], and your plans will succeed [if you respond to His will and guidance].*

Committing our ways to the Lord and obeying His leading sets us up for success. It allows our plans to be established and brings about the blessing of our God.

### 4. Prayer keeps us from temptation.

When Jesus was in the Garden of Gethsemane, He had asked His disciples to watch while He went to pray. When He came back, they were asleep. He asked in Matthew 26:40 (NIV):

*"Couldn't you men keep watch with me for one hour?"*

He went on to exhort them in Matthew 26:41 (NIV) to:

*"Watch and pray so that you will not fall into temptation. The spirit is willing, but the flesh is weak."*

Prayer protects us from falling into sin and temptation. Not yielding to temptation is one of the things that our prayers are to cover. Thus, we pray to strengthen ourselves since our flesh is weak.

### 5. Prayer builds us up in the faith.

Jude 20 says:

*But you, beloved, building yourselves up on your most holy faith, praying in the Holy Spirit,*

Prayer is a way to build our faith. The more we engage in this spiritual discipline, the stronger we will be. It is one way that we encourage ourselves in the Lord and achieve an intimacy with the One who is the Author and Finisher of our faith.

## 6. Prayer deepens our relationship with the Lord.

God longs to have intimacy with His children. He desires a relationship with us. He wants us to become familiar with Him, to truly know Him. He yearns for us to draw close to Him, spirit to Spirit. He desires our love and our time. He wants us to meet Him in the secret place.

Where is the secret place? It's in our spiritual "closet," which is not the one in our bedroom, but it is the secret dwelling place of our hearts where we can commune with Him. This is a place where we feel safe and protected from the world. We long to stay there forever because our secret hiding place is better shared with someone we love and trust. As we pursue relationship (communion) with God, that trust is built.

In Matthew 6:6, Jesus says:

> "But you, when you pray, go into your room, and when you have shut your door, pray to your Father who is in the secret place; and your Father who sees in secret will reward you openly."

Relationship has its rewards! Spending time in the secret place with God leads to benefits and blessings from our Heavenly Father.

### 7. Prayer equips us as Christian soldiers in the Army of God to be alert and ready.

The Christian soldier is compelled to be on constant guard duty. Why? Because the enemy never sleeps and constantly lurks to see whom he may devour. Thus, the Christian soldier must be on watch duty at all times and in all circumstances.

1 Peter 5:8 says:

*Be sober, be vigilant; because your adversary the devil walks about like a roaring lion, seeking whom he may devour.*

To be sober means 'to be discreet' and 'to watch'. In other words, it is an 'absence of sleep' that implies a wakeful frame of mind as opposed to passivity, carelessness, and apathy. In the spiritual sense, the commands to keep watch, be attentive, and be vigilant means to be fully awake to what is going on in the spiritual realm, not ignorant or unaware of the enemy's intent and tactics.

If one is to be calm in spirit, unemotional, and untouched by confusing circumstances, pitfalls, and outright attacks of the enemy, then watchfulness in prayer is necessary. In turn, prayer reinforces one's watchfulness, equipping believers to fight the good fight. Anything resembling unpreparedness or non-vigilance is death to prayer.

It is for this reason that a Christian soldier is to pray in all seasons and under all circumstances. Prayer and watchfulness go hand in hand. They are fundamental principles for all of Christ's warriors. We must always be alert!

When we sense the enemy coming, we can spiritually position ourselves in a way that says, "Halt! Who goes there?" Then, through our prayers and standing on the Word of God, we can send the enemy running!

All soldiers in God's army must be spiritually alert to the adversary's aggressive behavior and his tricks. He comes to steal, kill, and destroy. (John 10:10) A good soldier must always pray and not faint. (Luke 18:1, KJV)

It is also good to remember that there are others in the Army of God who can stand with us in prayer. Scripture tells us that there is power when Christians come together in prayer. (Matthew 18:19-20)

# Are you ready for duty?

Through Paul's writing in Ephesians 6:13-18, we are admonished as believers, as soldiers of Christ, to put on the whole armor of God:

*Therefore take up the whole armor of God, that you may be able to withstand in the evil day, and having done all, to stand. Stand therefore, having girded your waist with truth, having put on the breastplate of righteousness, and having shod your feet with the preparation of the gospel of peace; above all, taking the shield of faith with which you will be able to quench all the fiery darts of the wicked one. And take the helmet of salvation, and the sword of the Spirit, which is the word of God; praying always with all prayer and supplication in the Spirit, being watchful to this end with all perseverance and supplication for all the saints—*

This armor represents the virtues and the equipment necessary to defend the believer against Satan. These battles are spiritual in nature, and therefore, we need spiritual armor to be able to stand firm in the midst of these battles. In giving us the armor, God has fully equipped us to have victory over the enemy.

The armor of God includes the following pieces:

### 1. Belt of Truth

As the first item in a soldier's arsenal, the belt holds pieces of clothing and armor together. It secures the outfit and allows a soldier to move more freely.

One of Satan's greatest offensive tactics is to deceive us. With the belt of truth around our waist, we are prepared to defend ourselves against the enemy's maneuvers using the truth of the Word and what God has said. It allows us to stand in the face of lies and defeat the father of lies. Truth holds us together.

### 2. Breastplate of Righteousness

This piece covers our hearts and other vital organs. In other words, it covers our most vulnerable areas and those organs necessary for life. It is a defensive covering used for our protection.

Spiritually speaking, righteousness guards the believer's heart. The heart is the ruling center for the believer. As such, it is the righteousness within that defines or rules our lives as Christian soldiers, protecting our hearts and life.

### 3. Footwear of the Gospel of Peace

Outer footwear is used to protect the feet from rocks and thorns. It allows a person to tread on whatever ground is ahead of them with ease and stability.

The Christian soldier's boots are to be fitted with the readiness that comes from the gospel of peace. Because we know and truly grasp the Good News of Christ, that knowledge allows us to experience peace in Him no matter the circumstances. As a result, we can stand firm, able to withstand the attacks of the enemy because we know in Whom we have believed and are secure in Him.

## 4. Shield of Faith

The shield is a critical piece of armor used to deflect direct attacks of the enemy. It can be wielded to cover attacks from different angles as well as to protect vulnerable areas. Unlike a piece of armor that is strapped on and remains in one place, the shield must be intentionally used by the soldier bearing it, otherwise it is useless.

A strong faith covers us in all areas. It is the promised shield that quenches—as in completely snuffs out and makes ineffective— the darts the enemy throws at us.

## 5. Helmet of Salvation

The helmet protects another vulnerable part of the body—the head. Without the head, the body cannot operate.

What this means for us is that it protects our minds. There's a direct correlation in how we operate to what we entertain and meditate on in our thought lives. If our minds are compromised, we are ineffective in the battle and susceptible to attack.

It is through our salvation that our minds can be made sound, protected because of Jesus' work on the cross. Then, when the enemy looks into our eyes, he sees that we belong to Christ. Donning the helmet of salvation as a believer means that we continue to walk in the joy of our salvation by deliberately guarding our minds from being attacked by the enemy.

### 6. Sword of the Spirit

The sword is the one offensive weapon on the list. The purpose of the sword is to give us strength at the same time as it is used to inflict damage on the enemy.

The sword of the Spirit is the Word of God. Hebrews 4:12 tells us just how powerful this weapon is:

> *For the word of God is living and powerful, and sharper than any two-edged sword, piercing even to the division of soul and spirit, and of joints and marrow, and is a discerner of the thoughts and intents of the heart.*

The more we know and understand the Word, the more effective we will be against the enemy of our souls, able to withstand the evil onslaughts he launches against us. Not only will we be able to ward off the attacks Satan sends our way, but we can also wreak havoc on the forces of darkness.

### 7. Persistent Prayer and Praying in the Spirit

Ephesians 6:18 is a very important part of the fight against spiritual powers of evil. Let's review it again:

*praying always with all prayer and supplication in the Spirit, being watchful to this end with all perseverance and supplication for all the saints—*

Prayer may not be a recognized part of the armor, but it connects all the other pieces together and is an essential weapon in our spiritual battles against demonic forces. Without it, we are defeated.

As instructed, we are to pray *always*—at all times, on every occasion, in every season—with all prayers and supplications in the Spirit. Praying in the Spirit also means that we use the gift of tongues as part of our prayer life and strategy. Using prayer in this way, we draw strength from God and rely on Him to help us properly use the whole armor of God.

## Types of Prayers

Prayer can be frustrating if you don't understand God's Word concerning it. In addition, many Christians aren't aware that there are several types of prayers discussed in Scripture. God intended each form of prayer to serve a different purpose.

Remember that Ephesians 6:18 says that we are to pray at all times and on every occasion. Thus, for every time and occasion, there is a prayer that God has ordained to fit the situation. This information will help you to break the limitations off your prayer life.

## 1. The Prayer of Thanksgiving

The prayer of thanksgiving is gratitude directed towards God. Our thankfulness is expressed for personal reasons such as deliverance, God's faithfulness, and our forgiveness.

Psalms 100:4 tells us to:

> *Enter into His gates with thanksgiving, and into His courts with praise. Be thankful to Him, and bless His name.*

To enter in this context is a command. It isn't simply a description of the act of entering, but it is given as a directive, one that comes with specifics as to how we are to enter the Lord's presence.

Thanksgiving is derived from the verb *yadah*, meaning 'to give thanks' or 'to lift or extend the hands'. When we enter His gates—His presence—we do so through the extension of our hands in adoration to God with thanksgiving and a grateful heart. Thus, this is a prayer where we thank God for EVERTHING!

## 2. Prayer of Praise and Worship

Prayers of praise encompass a preoccupation with our blessings. It is the acknowledgment of God's perfection, works, and benefits. In this prayer, we are not asking Him to do or give us anything. We are not even asking for direction or dedicating our life to whatever it is God has called us to do. Rather, as Hebrews 13:15 says, we are to:

> ...continually offer the sacrifice of praise to God, that is, the fruit of our lips, giving thanks to His name.

What the Hebrew writer is saying here is that we are to offer praises to God continually with the fruit of our lips. The Greek word for lips is *cheilos*, which can be defined as 'a pouring place', meaning the pouring of words out of our mouths. This means we need to verbalize and pour forth our praises to Him.

We must not be afraid to deepen our praises to God by sharing with Him *all* that we exalt Him for. This is a sacrificial act on our part. "Lord, I praise You," or "I praise You for my job and my family," are good prayers, but they lack content or specifics. Getting specific takes the prayer of praise to a whole new level.

Psalms 95:6-7 says:

> Oh come, let us worship and bow down; Let us kneel before the Lord our Maker, for He is our God, and we are the people of His pasture, and the sheep of His hand...

Worship encompasses the preoccupation with God Himself. It is a surrendered attitude towards Him. It's when we revere Him, honor Him, fall prostrate before Him, and tell Him who He is. It's a celebration of the name of Jesus.

In addition, God desires that we give thanks to His name through praise and worship. The Greek word for giving thanks is *homologéo*, which means 'I confess', 'I publicly declare', or 'confession is made'. It also means 'to say the same thing as another', that is 'to agree with'. In other words, when we confess and publicly declare our thanks as part of prayers of praise and worship to God, we are saying what God says of Himself and come into agreement with Him. So, when we pray, we are to make confessions of what He says from the Scriptures and celebrate who He is and all that He has done.

### 3. Prayer of Supplication

Philippians 4:6 tells us:

> *Be anxious for nothing, but in everything by prayer and supplication, with thanksgiving, let your requests be made known to God;*

In supplication, the inner man is crying, requesting, pleading, and seeking earnestly for God to solve a dilemma. It's more than simply petitioning Him, for it communicates the intensity of a particular need or trial, transferring the heavy concern of one's soul over into God's hands and trusting Him to handle it.

## 4. Prayer of Faith

Mark 11:24 says:

*"Therefore I say to you, whatever things you ask when you pray, believe that you receive them, and you will have them."*

The prayer of faith is known as a petition prayer where one presents their needs and desires to the Lord. It's the prayer that most people think of when they hear the term "prayer." Petition prayer is between us and God, and it is when we ask God for a particular outcome.

God always answers prayer. However, we must make sure that we ask according to the Word of God and who He is. Otherwise, the answer will be "no" or we may experience a delay, for God does not violate His Word or His character. We can also be assured that He knows best, for as we learn in Ephesians 3:20, He does things *"exceedingly abundantly above all that we ask or think"* and His ways are higher than our ways. (Isaiah 55:9)

It is the prayer of faith that brings that answer out of the spiritual realm and into the physical world. Thus, when we pray, it must be something more than placing our hope in God's willingness and ability to do something for us. Instead, it is a definite, specific ask of the Lord in accordance with His Word, it is the complete belief that what He has said is true, it is accompanied by the fully persuaded expectation of the things for which we ask, and it is followed with corresponding actions that affirm one's faith. This includes positive declarations and claiming the promises found in the Word as our own. THIS is the prayer of faith.

## 5. Prayer of Healing

Jesus said in Matthew 10:8:

*"Heal the sick, cleanse the lepers, raise the dead, cast out demons. Freely you have received, freely give."*

We have been given all authority to heal the sick, cleanse the lepers (the untouchables), raise the dead, and cast out demons. This prayer taps into the supernatural on behalf of oneself or another person with the result manifesting in the natural. It is drawing from God's power in prayer based upon our covenant right and His Word.

The prayer of faith must accompany the prayer of healing. Our faith must be activated so that our prayers to heal the sick result in the manifestation of healing coming to pass.

## 6. Prayer of Intercession

Intercession is intervening on behalf of another. It is also interposing oneself between two parties and their difficulties or crises, usually through prayer. In addition, it is a means of aid, arbitration, or mediation. In the spiritual sense, it is imploring

God for His divine help, grace, mercy, and wisdom on behalf of others.

The Bible teaches that intercession is expected of all believers. In 1 Timothy 2:1-3, it reads:

> *Therefore I exhort first of all that supplications, prayers, intercessions, and giving of thanks be made for all men, for kings and all who are in authority, that we may lead a quiet and peaceable life in all godliness and reverence. For this is good and acceptable in the sight of God our Savior,*

It is important for us to follow this command, taking the time to pray for our families, friends, and others. In addition, it is part of our mandate to intercede for those in authority over us, to pray for leaders, governments, for countries and nations, for Israel, and more. We are literally to be ready to intercede for anyone and everyone that God puts on our hearts to pray for.

God finds our prayers of intercession to be *"good and acceptable"* before Him. With Holy Spirit's help, the believer who is burdened under the prayer of intercession will be able to carry even undefinable prayers to God for His care and attention.

### 7.  Prayer of Agreement

This type of prayer is also a promise given by Jesus to all believers. He said in Matthew 18:19-20:

> *"Again I say to you that if two of you agree on earth concerning anything that they ask, it will be done for them by My Father in heaven. For where two or three are gathered together in My name, I am there in the midst of them."*

Many have misinterpreted this Scripture and thought it was about touching one another as we pray. That is not what Jesus meant. Touching is not necessary. The prayer of agreement is about being in one accord, of one mind, and harmonizing together in agreement about that which is being prayed for. The promise is that He will grant us our petition while being in our midst.

### 8.  Prayer of Binding and Loosing

Jesus said in Matthew 18:18:

> *"Assuredly, I say to you, whatever you bind on earth will be bound in heaven, and whatever you loose on earth will be loosed in heaven."*

There are several important nuggets to be drawn from Jesus' statement here, the first one being that we have authority here on this earth by virtue of our covenant rights through Jesus. The second thing we notice is the direction of the action. Things do not begin in heaven and come to earth, but rather the action starts here on earth then goes to heaven.

Like all things in God's system, this type of prayer works only in line with God's Word and His laws. Otherwise, this turns into cursing. Therefore, we must be very careful to make sure that we only bind and loose that which is in agreement with the Word and what God has said.

### 9. Praying in the Spirit

I have mentioned Ephesians 6:18 already, but let's review the first part of the verse once again:

> *praying always with all prayer and supplication in the Spirit...*

Praying *"in the Spirit"* (also known as speaking in tongues) causes us to become more conscious of God. Additionally, it is a vitally important part in the fight against spiritual evil powers.

When we pray in the Spirit, it can be likened to charging a car battery. It acts like spiritual jumper cables that connect us to our Heavenly Power Source. This enables us to be filled back up so that we can operate at our best and be useful.

We already learned in Jude 20 how praying in the Holy Spirit helps us to build ourselves up in our faith. It fills us with His power that we may be ready for the Master's use. We all can use this type of jump start in our prayer life. All of us need this boost!

### 10. Corporate Prayer

Corporate prayer is when members of the Body of Christ come together to present prayers, petitions, and supplications to the Lord. It is a gathering together before the Lord as the Church for a specific reason including intercession.

In 2 Chronicles 7:14, God said:

> *"if My people who are called by My name will humble themselves, and pray and seek My face, and turn from their wicked ways, then I will hear from heaven, and will forgive their sin and heal their land."*

Contextually, this Scripture points to the conversation God had with Solomon after the dedication of the temple. God had heard Solomon's prayer and said in 2 Chronicles 7:13, *"When I shut up heaven and there is no rain, or command the locusts to devour the land, or send pestilence among My people"*. It was then that He went on to say what He did in 2 Chronicles 7:14 about His people humbly coming together to pray.

Drastic and turbulent times unleashed upon society have often required a corporate response in prayer. In our modern society, we also experience disasters, diseases, poverty, and extreme need. Therefore, we, too, have the need to practice corporate prayer. And if the "Called Out Ones"—a.k.a. the Church—would humble themselves and pray and seek His face, God will hear us and will answer our prayers just like He promised Solomon.

However, God's promise to answer this prayer is determined on the condition of IF. IF means 'granted that, provided that, on condition that'. So, IF certain conditions are met, the fulfillment of what we have corporately asked for in prayer will be granted.

The first condition is that we must humble ourselves. Christian humility is the grace that makes one think of him- or herself no more highly than he or she ought to think. It requires us to recognize that, outside of God's righteousness and what Jesus did on the cross, we *are* nothing. This humility acknowledges that God is all-powerful and without Him, we can *do* nothing. Thus, we exhibit a spirit of humility or meekness in our asking of the Lord.

Secondly, we must earnestly pray. Our spiritual life depends on our communication with the Lord, but in corporate prayer, we are going before the Lord with concerns that affect the Body, the world, and generations to come. We are interceding for many.

Thirdly, we are to seek God's face. Seeking His face means that we align ourselves to what God wants. We need His wisdom, His intervention, His hand to move miraculously, and more. As such, we go to Him from that place of relationship and petition Him directly.

And finally, we absolutely must turn from our wicked ways. This means that genuine repentance is required. Our own hearts must be cleansed before we can receive what we are petitioning God for in addition to His mercy.

Obedience in meeting these conditions is critically important. IF we obey, God WILL hear from Heaven, forgive our sins, and heal our land.

### 11. Prayer of Repentance and Forgiveness

Prayers of repentance may be a requirement of corporate prayer, but it is also a type of prayer that we employ when coming to the Lord on our own. It is coupled with a genuine recognition of where we have sinned, and it involves asking for forgiveness.

King David expressed deep sorrow for his sin with Bathsheba. His prayer of repentance is recorded in Psalms 51. Verses 2-3 say:

> *Wash me thoroughly from my iniquity, and cleanse me from my sin. For I acknowledge my transgressions, and my sin is always before me.*

He goes on to pray in verses 10-12:

> *Create in me a clean heart, O God, and renew a steadfast spirit within me. Do not cast me away from Your presence, and do not take Your Holy Spirit from me.*

*Restore to me the joy of Your salvation, and uphold me*
*by Your generous Spirit.*

King David's plea to the Father was one of true repentance, one that asked for forgiveness, for his sins to be blotted out. (v. 9) He approached the Lord with a humbleness of heart, fully acknowledging the need for deliverance and forgiveness. We are to be just as sincere in coming to God with our sin.

### 12. Prayer for Grace and Mercy

Prayer for God's grace and mercy are often incorporated as part of our prayers of supplication, faith, healing, intercession, repentance and forgiveness, and in times of corporate prayer. This prayer specifically requests God's grace and mercy to be released to answer a particular need.

In Hebrews 4:16, we read:

*Let us come boldly before the throne of grace, that we*
*may obtain mercy and grace to help in time of need.*

This type of prayer is about coming into God's presence with boldness, earnestly seeking His help, wisdom, and strategy. We need His grace to enable us to be who we have been called to be and operate effectively in our calling. We need His mercy, not just for the forgiveness of sin, but to comfort us and bring relief in times of distress.

Knowing what prayer is, why we are to pray, and the purpose behind each type of prayer changes how we approach this spiritual discipline. We can be much more effective in our prayer life when we have this understanding and insight. There is POWER in prayer once we have this knowledge and implement it.

As we conclude this chapter, I encourage you to invest in your prayer life *today.* Examine how much time you spend in prayer.

- Do you start your day with prayer?
- What are your prayer habits?
- Do you only approach the Lord in certain circumstances?
- What is holding you back from engaging in conversations with God?

Answer these questions and any other questions the Lord brings to your mind. Then, ask yourself and the Lord about what you need to change to incorporate the power of prayer into your life. I promise you...it will be worth it!

# CHAPTER SEVEN
# The Power of Corporate Praise

Praise comes from a Latin word meaning 'attach value to' or 'set a price on'. When we praise something or someone, it is the result of the high value that thing or person has. Therefore, praise is the approval or acknowledgment of the prize or worth found in its object. It is also an expression of admiration, gratitude, and devotion, especially for blessings received.

When applying this to our relationship with God, praise is one of humanity's many responses to God's revelation of Himself. Praise to God is the acknowledgement of His perfection, works, and benefits. Praise properly culminates the focus on God on account of His natural excellences and perfection. It is an act of devotion by which we confess and admire His numerous attributes. We praise God for all His glorious acts of every kind, including those that involve others and not just ourselves. Therefore, to give praise to God is to proclaim His merit or worth.

Many terms are used to express praise in the Bible. These include 'glory', 'blessing', 'thanksgiving', and 'hallelujah'. The term 'hallelujah' is a combination of two Hebrew words meaning 'praise to God'. The Hebrew title of the book of Psalms literally means 'praises'.

Praise is invariably linked to music, both instrumental and vocal. Biblical songs of praise range from personal to corporate and often include spontaneous outbursts of thanksgiving for some redemptive act of God.

Paul instructs the Church in Ephesians 5:18-19:

> *And do not be drunk with wine, in which is dissipation; but be filled with the Spirit, speaking to one another in psalms and hymns and spiritual songs, singing and making melody in your heart to the Lord,*

Paul declares that praises and worship to God are a natural part of living the Spirit-filled life. Our praise and worship are commonly expressed in song.

Praise is to originate from the heart. It is not meant to become a mere outward show. Instead, our hearts must be aligned with our lips as we express our praise and worship to God.

Jesus said in Matthew 15:8-9 (AMPC):

> *These people draw near Me with their mouths and honor Me with their lips, but their hearts hold off and are far away from Me. Uselessly do they worship Me, for they teach as doctrines the commands of men.*

No study of praise or worship would be complete without considering the practical expression of corporate worship, especially as set forth in God's Word. While it is the heart of the individual believer that must respond to God in worship, it is the corporate Church that represents the revelation of Christ most fully on the earth. Through our praise and worship, particularly when corporately expressed, we see and experience many benefits.

## 1. Victory

There is victory in using our corporate praises as a weapon in battle, for God inhabits the praises of His people. When we praise and worship Him in spirit and in truth, His presence descends among us, bringing the presence of God to fill every situation that we are facing in life. This sets us up to be victorious.

In 2 Chronicles 20, Jehoshaphat was facing a great battle. He sought the Lord and proclaimed a fast for all the people. In their prayers, they kept their eyes on God. The Lord heard their cry and promised them victory. The prophetic word given was to not be afraid or dismayed. God let them know that the battle was not theirs but His. He told them to *"Position yourselves, stand still and see the salvation of the Lord...tomorrow go out against them, for the Lord is with you."* (v. 17)

In response, Jehoshaphat sent singers and worshipers ahead of his army. They were singing in the beauty of holiness, *"Praise the Lord, for His mercy endures forever."* (v. 21) As they praised and worshiped, the Lord caused the enemies to fight each other and destroy themselves. Because Jehoshaphat and the people positioned themselves through praise and worship, they didn't have to fight. They saw the salvation of the Lord.

This same truth applies to us today. God gives us strategic instructions for the fight against the enemy as we praise and worship Him. When we praise and worship the Lord in our battles, this causes confusion in the camp of the enemy and causes them to destroy themselves. Thus, our praise and worship positions us to triumph over the enemy, and the Lord becomes our victory.

There is power in praise! There is victory in praise!

## 2. Breakthrough

Praise is the pathway to our breakthrough. When we praise and worship, we posture ourselves to experience breakthrough in our lives and see the hindrances to our blessings removed.

When Joshua was facing the wall of Jericho, the Lord instructed the children of Israel in Joshua 6 to walk silently around the city for six days, but then on the seventh day, they were to make a great shout—shouts of praise unto the Lord. These praise shouts served as a battle cry, and the wall came tumbling down.

When we praise and worship, walls of resistance come down. As a result, a way is made to enter into the promises of God for our lives.

### 3. Freedom

In Acts 16:23-26, Paul and Silas were beaten repeatedly, bound, and thrown into prison. In the midst of their pain and bondage, they didn't murmur or complain. Instead, they began to pray and sing hymns to God. *Suddenly,* there was an earthquake that shook the foundations of the prison. This caused all the doors to be opened, and everyone's chains were loosed.

When we praise and worship from the heart, we experience freedom from bondage. There is power in praise that can be realized even in our most difficult circumstances. Praise from the heart directed to God opens prison doors.

Do you desire a "suddenly" experience? Begin to praise and worship God in your pain and in your bondage. This sets you up for the "suddenlies" of God to happen in your life and bring freedom.

### 4. Deliverance

Praise and worship prepare us to be delivered from demonic oppression. King Saul was tormented by an evil spirit as we read about in 1 Samuel 16:14-23. So, they brought David to play the harp before him. David was a worshiper, and as he played the harp and worshiped the Lord, the evil spirit departed from Saul. He was refreshed and made well.

This demonstrates why we need anointed worship leaders, singers, and musicians in our church services. Many people that attend the services need deliverance. They may be plagued with evil spirits such as fear, doubt, and unbelief. An anointed worshiper will help drive those evil spirits out. Pure praise and worship will help fill each person with faith as the greatness of God is extolled. Thus, we need people who are not about the performance of it all but who possess a heart for God as true worshipers.

## 5. Revelation

When the kings of Israel, Judah, and Edom went to battle against the King of Moab, they faced great danger upon running out of water for their troops. They sought the mind of the Lord through the prophet Elisha.

Elisha called for a musician to play before him. As the musician played and worshiped, the hand of the Lord came upon Elisha, and he received revelation from God for His people. The Lord provided the water they needed, and He also promised them victory in the battle. (See 2 Kings 3:1-20)

Sincere praise and worship offered up to the Lord will open the door for us to receive revelation of God's will and purpose for our lives. That revelation prepares the way for provision and victory.

## 6. Judgment

In Psalms 149:6-9, we read about the *"high praises of God"* bringing down the judgment of God upon evildoers. Through our praises, we can bind the forces of wickedness from carrying out their destructive activities against us. The Lord responds to our praises by vindicating us, rendering justice on our behalf, and enforcing His divine vengeance on our foes.

## 7. Healing

When we praise and worship from the heart, we experience healing and miracles in our lives. Let's look at a few examples...

The leper who *worshiped* Jesus was healed from his leprosy. (Matthew 8:1-3)

> *When He had come down from the mountain, great multitudes followed Him. And behold, a leper came and worshiped Him, saying, "Lord, if You are willing, You can make me clean."*
>
> *Then Jesus put out His hand and touched him, saying, "I am willing; be cleansed." Immediately his leprosy was cleansed.*

The ruler who *worshiped* Jesus had his daughter raised from the dead. (Matthew 9:18-19, 23-26)

*While He spoke these things to them, behold, a ruler came and worshiped Him, saying, "My daughter has just died, but come and lay Your hand on her and she will live." So Jesus arose and followed him, and so did His disciples.*

*When Jesus came into the ruler's house, and saw the flute players and the noisy crowd wailing, He said to them, "Make room, for the girl is not dead, but sleeping." And they ridiculed Him. But when the crowd was put outside, He went in and took her by the hand, and the girl arose. And the report of this went out into all that land.*

The Canaanite woman who *worshiped* Jesus received deliverance for her daughter from demon possession. (Matthew 15:21-28)

*Then Jesus went out from there and departed to the region of Tyre and Sidon. And behold, a woman of Canaan came from that region and cried out to Him, saying, "Have mercy on me, O Lord, Son of David! My daughter is severely demon-possessed."*

*But He answered her not a word. And His disciples came and urged Him, saying, "Send her away, for she cries out after us."*

*But He answered and said, "I was not sent except to the lost sheep of the house of Israel."*

*Then she came and worshiped Him, saying, "Lord, help me!"*

*But He answered and said, "It is not good to take the children's bread and throw it to the little dogs."*

*And she said, "Yes, Lord, yet even the little dogs eat the crumbs which fall from their masters' table."*

*Then Jesus answered and said to her, "O woman, great is your faith! Let it be to you as you desire." And her daughter was healed from that very hour.*

In these three accounts from the book of Matthew, all worshiped Jesus. Their worship moved the heart of the Son of God to act on their behalf and bring healing.

I am glad that the Lord Jesus is always willing to come and heal. He longs to help the sick. He loves to heal us of our afflictions.

Therefore, when we praise and worship the Lord in the midst of our pain and suffering, the Lord is moved with compassion. He will perform miracles in our lives if only we believe.

Offering up praise and worship to God is a command found all throughout Scripture. Even though it applies to us individually, it is also a corporate responsibility of God's people. As we have seen, the power of corporate praise moves the hand of God to supernaturally act on our behalf, even to the changing of nations. As a result, the light of God shines through us when we offer up our high praises to God here on earth.

## CHAPTER EIGHT

The Pattern

From the beginning, God has yearned for mankind to fellowship with Him, worship Him, and come into His presence. He walked in the Garden of Eden in the cool of each evening just to commune with the first man and woman. They were in His presence daily. That was the original plan of God for the human race. It was the way we were created to live—to be in an intimate relationship with God, fellowshipping with Him daily.

Then, the Fall happened, and sin separated humanity from God. Because of the Fall:

- We no longer had direct access to Him.

- We no longer could dwell in His presence.

- We no longer had fellowship with Him.

- We no longer had an intimate relationship with Him.

However, in His infinite wisdom and since He is omniscient (all-knowing), God foreknew that man would sin. So, His fore-ordained plan went into motion, one that made a way for people to get back to the place where they could walk in fellowship with Him once again.

You see, the passion of God's heart is to be in close relationship with us. He longs to be to us what He was to Adam and Eve before the Fall. Think about it! God deeply desires to *BE with us!*

We may not understand it fully, and we may not even be aware of it, but there is a passion in all our hearts to be where God is. God made us to be innately that way, and that desire is never satisfied until we are in His presence. It's a universal human need.

Therefore, every believer has the desire to fellowship with God. Deep down, they want to have a powerful, daily devotional time with Him, one that intimately connects them with the Most High.

As part of this connection with God, we were also created by Him to be worshipers. The issue is not whether we're going to worship or not. Instead, it is a question of *whom* or *what* we're going to worship.

We know from both biblical and secular history that people have worshiped idols. They have built inanimate objects like the golden calf or some other creature or figurehead, and they have bowed down and worshiped it. Even in the modern age, this type of worship is practiced in areas of the world.

Today, men and women are still searching to find someone or something to worship. Everyone, even the worst sinner in the world, is a worshiper. People may idolize their career, money, sex, a political system, or power. This is simply another form of worship. Ultimately, we make the decision as to whom or what we worship.

The drive inside of us to worship is rooted in the hunger to find God, to be where He is. Neither career, money, sex, nor power can fulfill the longing and desire we experience in our hearts. Only when we meet God do we find an answer to that longing inside. Only when we worship Him and sit in His presence are we truly content. Only then is that hunger for fellowship and desire to be with God satisfied.

I can only imagine how much it hurts God when we don't worship Him as a true worshiper. Too often, believers have become spectators, watching how others praise and worship but not entering in ourselves. Others go through the motions, offering up their praises without thought or a genuineness of heart. I truly believe this grieves the heart of God.

## How to Worship

Jesus said in John 4:23:

> *"But the hour is coming, and now is, when the true worshipers will worship the Father in spirit and truth; for the Father is seeking such to worship Him."*

This is such a powerful verse. Think about it! The Father genuinely seeks us to worship Him. This seeking speaks of His deep desire and search for a people with whom to have fellowship, a people who will adore Him as the loving and mighty God that He is.

Note that this verse also defines what a true worshiper is. It is defined as one who worships *"in spirit and truth"*. For us, this means that our worship must be genuine and sincere, originating from the heart. It involves our whole being in response to who God is.

Thus, the Lord is seeking those who have fervently adopted the lifestyle and mindset of a worshiper. And He has not left us without help or direction, for the Bible teaches us many ways of how to worship Him.

## 1. We worship God with our bodies.

When we bow down, kneel, or lay prostrate on the floor, these are acts of worship as we read about in Psalms 95:6 where it states, *"Oh come, let us worship and bow down; let us kneel before the Lord our Maker."*

The Bible talks about worshiping the Lord through the lifting of our hands. Psalms 134:2 tells us to *"Lift up your hands in the sanctuary, and bless the Lord."* Psalms 63:4 says, *"Thus I will bless You while I live; I will lift up my hands in Your name."*

We also can worship the Lord through dance and the movement of our whole bodies. In Psalms 149:3a, the psalmist writes, *"Let them praise His name with the dance..."*

## 2. We are to worship God in song.

In Psalms 100:2 in the NIV, we read that we are to *"Worship the Lord with gladness; come before him with joyful songs."* Notice that these songs come from a heart of joy and gladness.

## 3. We are to worship God with musical instruments.

Along with singing songs, musical instruments are regularly associated with worship. In fact, the use of instruments in worship was practiced long before our modern-day services. As we read in 2 Chronicles 29:28a, *"The whole assembly bowed in worship, while the musicians played and the trumpets sounded..."* (NIV) Psalms 150 talks about letting all things praise the Lord, including using musical instruments. Verses 3-5 state, *"Praise Him with the sound of the trumpet; Praise Him with the lute and harp! Praise Him with the timbrel and dance; Praise Him with the stringed instruments and flutes! Praise Him with loud cymbals; Praise Him with clashing cymbals!"*

## 4. We are to worship God with the right attitude.

We are not to take our worship of the Lord lightly! He is holy and mighty and awesome in power. He is worthy of all our praises and adoration. Therefore, we are to *"worship God acceptably with reverence and awe"* as we are instructed in Hebrews 12:28. (NIV) This reverence and awe flows from a place of deep respect and humility towards God.

### 5. We are to worship God through our offerings.

In 1 Chronicles 16:29, we are commanded to *"Give to the Lord the glory due His name; bring an offering, and come before Him. Oh, worship the Lord in the beauty of holiness!"* Thus, bringing an offering before the Lord is an act of worship.

### 6. We are to worship God with our lives.

A lifestyle of worship involves our entire lives offered up as a living sacrifice to the Lord. We read about this in Romans 12:1 (NIV), which states, *"Therefore, I urge you, brothers and sisters, in view of God's mercy, to offer your bodies as a living sacrifice, holy and pleasing to God—this is your true and proper worship."*

## Worship is learned.

We must learn the art of expressing ourselves to God in worship. We must learn how to open our hearts as channels of the Holy Spirit. Thus, our ability to worship must be developed through application and experience.

It is important to take our growth as true worshipers seriously. In addition to studying the Word of God, our main source, we can also develop our worship by reading books, taking classes, or going to seminars. Being part of a church community and around godly leaders who understand the importance of the expression of worship is highly beneficial as well. The bottom line is, *we* are responsible for our own growth as true worshipers, seeking out that which increases our knowledge on the subject, and putting into practice what we have learned.

## Worship is about relationship.

If we are not worshiping, obviously there's no relationship with the Lord. Without relationship, there's no attitude of deep respect for Him. Without relationship, we don't reverence Him as the Lord of our lives. Relationship is required to become a true worshiper of God.

As we learn to enjoy a relationship with God out of a thankful and surrendered heart that praises Him, reverence for God begins to displace worldly attitudes and deter us from ungodly pursuits. Our proud hearts are humbled, and we experience true gratitude for God's goodness to us, which is so undeserved. As a result, it becomes natural for us to respond to His goodness through worship.

# Obedience and Submission

Without a heart of obedience and submission to the Word of God, we will never experience true worship in spirit and in truth. Obedience and submission are part of our learning as well as our relationship with God. They must be practiced daily.

Now, some people may think they have to be holy first before they can enter into God's presence. The problem with that mentality is that, if a person has sinned, guilt and shame tend to surface and become dominant. As a result, that person is not inclined to pray or worship God because their thoughts will be along the lines of, "I'm not holy enough." This is not God's heart for His people. God wants all of us to come as we are and worship Him.

You might say, "Okay, I have this area of sin that I struggle with. How do I break it? I try to resist, but I keep falling."

I want to make a very important point here. When we were yet unsaved, we were sinners. Once we have received the Lord, we have been made righteous. No longer are we to be sin conscious. Instead, we are the righteous who occasionally struggle with sin versus sinners trying to be made righteous through our own efforts. We have been made holy through the work of the cross.

Therefore, if we are struggling in an area, repentance is key to turning it around and walking in the righteousness that is already ours. In addition, the Bible says in James 4:7 to *"submit to God. Resist the devil and he will flee from you."*

Many people only focus on the second part of that verse, which is *"resist the devil and he will flee from you."* In their own strength, they try to resist...but instead, they keep falling into sin. However, the key to resisting the devil is to *"submit to God"*.

So, submitting to God comes first. Submission is an act of obedience that allows us to walk in complete obedience daily. This leads to us becoming full of God's empowering grace through praising and worshiping Him, resulting in His glory coming down on us. At this point, we have enough of God's strength to resist the enemy.

As part of this walk of obedience and submission to God, I encourage you to pray and always to repent of any wrongdoing and as the Holy Spirit convicts. Ask God to forgive you and wash you thoroughly. Be filled with God's glory. Be stuffed with His presence and with His joy. And when sin comes knocking, don't answer the door, and the intruder *will* flee.


## The Pattern of the Tabernacle

Next, I will explain how to enter into God's presence using the pattern God gave Moses in the Old Testament. This pattern was given so that the Israelites could understand how to come into His presence.

In the building of the tabernacle, God made a way so that His glory could dwell among men. Today, we are meant to experience that same glory. Unfortunately, many have strayed away from God-ordained worship, which is to be expressed in a similar matter as it was in the first tabernacle. As a result, people have failed to move closer to God's ultimate purpose for their lives. It is time to change that.

Now, Paul shed light on the ultimate purpose of the human body when he admonished the brethren in 2 Corinthians 6:16. He said:

> And what agreement has the temple of God with idols? For you are the temple of the living God. As God has said: "I will dwell in them and walk among them. I will be their God, and they shall be My people."

There is a purpose behind everything God does. In creating the human body, He designed it to become a temple for God, growing in the righteous character of God. Thus, through His dwelling in us by the power of the Holy Spirit, we are helped in achieving this purpose and enabled to live forever as part of His family.

The pattern established in the Old Testament tabernacle is the spiritual pattern for us to follow. It encompasses how to enter God's presence and what our worship should be all about. Many people have not understood that we, the Church, are now the temple or tabernacle of the Most Hight God. We are, indeed, the New Testament temples where God desires to dwell.

When we enter God's presence, something special happens. Not only do we experience worship and fellowship, but we begin to receive Jehovah's revelation knowledge. We see powerful, spiritual truths that will heal us and bless us in our marriages, our family, our finances, our relationships, and every other aspect of our lives. As the psalmist writes in Psalms 16:11, *"In Your presence is fullness of joy"*.

If you have a desire to really know God and be in His presence, take the opportunity to learn this pattern. Then, you will be able to handle anything that comes your way.

Now, let's begin our journey!

## 1. The Introduction of the Tabernacle

There are a few synonyms that name or describe the tabernacle. They include:

- The dwelling place
- House of God – a fixed, settled habitation
- Place of sanctity – the holy, consecrated place
- Sanctuary
- The Temple – the stately building or palace of Jehovah

- Tabernacle of the congregation

- Tabernacle of the covenant law

- Tabernacle of Testimony

- Tabernacle (or tent) of meeting

These different terms all refer to the tabernacle where God's people went to meet Him.

## 2. The Three Tabernacles of the Old Testament

*The Provisional Tabernacle* was established after the Israelite's sin of creating the golden calf. During this period, Moses would take his tent and pitch it outside the camp, calling it the *"tabernacle of meeting."* It was the place for God's presence to descend, a place where He could be inquired of. In this temporary tabernacle, there were no rituals, no furnishings, and no priesthood. When Moses entered this tent of meeting, the Lord would talk to him face to face. In response to the pillar of cloud descending and standing at the door of the tabernacle— God's presence—the people would rise and worship. (See Exodus 33:7-11)

*The Sinaitic Tabernacle* was erected according to directions given to Moses by Jehovah and positioned at the center of the camp. (See Exodus 25-40) It was portable so that the Israelites could carry it through the wilderness.

*The Davidic Tabernacle* was erected by David in Jerusalem for the reception of the Ark of the Covenant. (See 2 Samuel 6:17)

### 3. More on the Sinaitic Tabernacle

After Israel's sin of building the golden calf in the wilderness, and after Moses interceded on their behalf, Jehovah renewed His covenant with Israel, gave them another copy of the law, and invited them to make offerings of material and resources for the construction of a new tabernacle. The people responded by giving in excess of what was asked for. (See Exodus 36:3-5)

This new tabernacle was set up on the first day of the first month. According to the Jewish calendar, it was the month of Nisan, which is our April. The Lord commanded Moses to place the Ark of the Testimony (or Covenant) inside the Most Holy Place and install an inner curtain to enclose the Ark. A table was to be brought in and things arranged on it in a specific order, plus there was a golden lampstand that had special meaning and gave light. Unlike the Provisional Tabernacle, which was placed outside the camp, the Sinaitic Tabernacle stood in the center of the camp. (See Exodus 40:1-5)

## 4. Key Areas of the Tabernacle

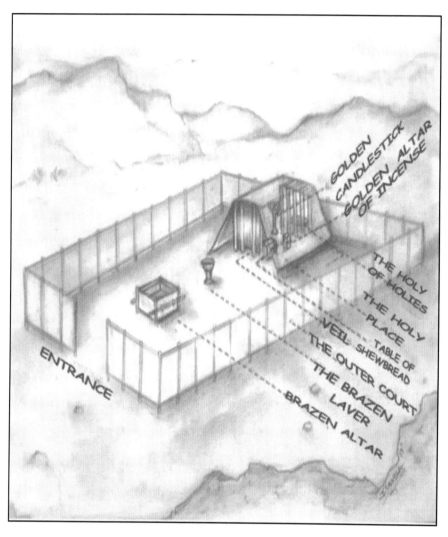

The entire tabernacle was composed of three distinct areas: the outer court, the Holy Place, and the Holy of Holies. First, the outer court was created by a linen curtain "wall" that enclosed the entire tent of meeting. Inside this curtained wall was a two-compartment tent. The first space was called the Holy Place, and it was separated from the second compartment by a thick curtain or veil. The second space was called the Holy of Holies (the Most Holy Place), the place where the presence of God dwelt. The actual glory of God dwelt in a cloud over the mercy seat on top of the Ark of the Covenant inside the Holy of Holies. These were the three key areas of the tabernacle.

When we look at this pattern of the tabernacle, it is important to understand how it applies to our lives today. We must look for how God established the tabernacle to lay a foundation and principles for us to follow. Specifically, the pattern provides a parallel for how we as believers are to enter into His presence.

First, it shows us that there are dimensions in our journey of pursuing God. As we walk in relationship, it is part of our purpose to grow in our intimacy and fellowship with the Most High.

Secondly, it is imperative that we reach the third dimension—that Most Holy Place—in our walk with God. This is the place where God hears and answers our prayers while we are in His presence. Receiving answers to our prayers does not come by luck, chance, or our own ability to pray. They come through our faith, our trust, and our willingness to wait and listen to God's still small voice. Answers come through cultivating a close relationship with God, a relationship that leads to having the heart of a true worshiper.

When we continue to examine all the special facts connected with the Sinaitic Tabernacle in the Bible, God's purpose clearly appears. The bottom line is, it was the place where man met with God. In the same manner, it is the special and intimate place where He desires us to be...IN HIS PRESENCE! Can you feel Him tugging on your heart to take this journey?

Before any of us can enter the outer court, though, we must first walk through the gate.

## 5.  The Gate into the Outer Court

In both the Hebrew and Greek, gate means 'opening door' or 'entrance'. This gate opened into the enclosed grounds or courtyard that was considered the outer court of the tabernacle. It represents the introductory stage of our relationship with the Lord, particularly in the area of prayer.

The twelve tribes of Israel were camped around the outside of the tabernacle's outer wall. Each tribe had been given a specific location to pitch their tents. Regardless of a tribe's location, every Israelite had to enter the outer courtyard through the same gate.

This leads to my first main point. In Ephesians 2:11-12, the Apostle Paul describes the desperate condition of the Gentiles before the death of Jesus:

*Therefore remember that you, once Gentiles in the flesh—who are called Uncircumcision by what is called the Circumcision made in the flesh by hands—that at that time you were without Christ, being aliens from the commonwealth of Israel and strangers from the covenants of promise, having no hope and without God in the world.*

However, through the sacrifice of Jesus at Calvary, ALL were made alike, having access to God and an intimate relationship with Him.

Paul continues in verse 13, saying:

*But now in Christ Jesus you who once were far off have been brought near by the blood of Christ.*

Through Jesus' death and resurrection, we ALL enter through the same "gate" of salvation and reconciliation to God. This is very important to remember.

Next, what is so important about this gate when it comes to our prayer life and relationship with God?

Jesus said in John 10:7-10,

*..."Most assuredly, I say to you, I am the door of the sheep. All who ever came before Me are thieves and robbers, but the sheep did not hear them. I am the door. If anyone enters by Me, he will be saved, and will go in*

and out and find pasture. The thief does not come except to steal, and to kill, and to destroy. I have come that they may have life, and that they may have it more abundantly."

And in John 14:6, Jesus says:

... "I am the way, the truth, and the life. No one comes to the Father except through Me."

The door or gate signifies that Jesus is the only way into the presence of God. We must all go through the gate of Jesus. We cannot enter the Holy of Holies and that place of intimate fellowship with God without going through Jesus first.

Non-believers cannot experience the presence of God. They have not yet accepted the works of Jesus Christ and what He did on the cross. He is the Way, the Truth, and the Life, the One who leads us to the very presence of the Most High God. Until non-believers come to that saving knowledge of Jesus Christ and accept Him as Lord and Savior and pray believing, they will not experience the indwelling presence of God.

However, Jesus' heart is for the non-believer to come to Him and be saved so that they may fully enter into and experience God's presence.

According to Luke 5:32, Jesus tells us:

"I have not come to call the righteous, but sinners, to repentance."

We are also reminded in 2 Peter 3:9b that the Lord is *"not willing that any should perish but that all should come to repentance."* Therefore, to pass through the gate, we must accept His works as part of our lives.

The next point I want to make is that to enter into the things of God, we must be thankful for what He has done as we read about in Psalms 100:4:

> *Enter into His gates with thanksgiving, and into His courts with praise. Be thankful to Him, and bless His name.*

Start with thanksgiving. Thank God for what He's done in the past. When I think about all that God has done for me, I can't help but say, "Thank you, Jesus!"

Before we enter the outer court, I want you to understand that God works in threes. Some examples are:

- Father, Son, Holy Spirit
- Outer court, Holy Place, Holy of Holies
- The Way, the Truth, the Life
- Spirit, soul, body
- God's attributes: omniscient, omnipresent, omnipotent
- Three divisions of time: past, present, future
- Jesus was anointed: Prophet, Priest, King

The significance of three is that it means 'divine perfection'. God is perfect in all His ways.

Now, I want you to especially notice the three parts we have as humans—we are spirit, soul, and body. This is significant when applying the pattern of the tabernacle to our own lives where WE are the temple of God.

First, the spirit represents our inner man. This is the most important part of who we are. With our spirit, we are God-breathed, enabled to be God-conscious.

Secondly, we possess a soul, which is comprised of our mind, will, intelligence, and emotions. We are aware of ourselves as a unique creation of God through our soul. This makes us self-conscious.

Finally, we have a physical body. Our bodies have five senses—touch, taste, smell, sight, and hearing. These five senses enable us to experience the world around us, which makes us world conscious.

We cannot comprehend God through our bodies or our souls. Instead, we experience Him through the new birth that happens in our spirits. This transformation begins when we enter through the gate of Jesus.

These three parts of a person relate directly to the pattern of the tabernacle.

- The body is the outer court.

- The soul is the Holy Place.

- The spirit is the Holy of Holies.

Thus, the final point I want to make is that we must learn to move from the outer court (our flesh) to the Holy Place (our soul) to the Holy of Holies (our spirit) because God exists only in the spirit realm. It is through our spirits that we enter into and experience His presence. There are also three levels to approaching God and pursuing His presence: thanksgiving, praise, and worship. Each one is a progressive step to the next.

Are you ready for this journey?

# CHAPTER NINE

# The Journey

## The Outer Court

According to the pattern of the tabernacle, once a person entered through the gate into the outer court, they saw an altar of sacrifice. It was upon this altar that blood sacrifices were made in atonement for sin. The act of sacrificing an animal to atone for sin stood for the future death and blood sacrifice of Jesus. Upon Jesus' death and resurrection, the New Covenant was ushered in, abolishing the need for blood sacrifices since the required atonement was satisfied once and for all. For us today, entering through the gate of Jesus allows us to become partakers of the benefits of His sacrifice.

Now, the tabernacle's court was enclosed by fabric walls but open to the air and lit by natural sunlight. In a similar manner, when we enter the court of our God, we are given eternal light through the plan of salvation. However, we haven't yet received eternal *revelation*. We are still under the influence of natural light. So even though we are saved, we are constantly being exposed to natural elements (the carnal world, secular influences, etc.). Therefore, if we remain in the outer court, fleshly opinions, worldly beliefs, and earthly circumstances will hinder our pursuit of God.

The people of Israel gathered in the outer court. They discussed their opinions about God and other things too. When those conversations turned to murmuring—complaining to each other about what they "thought" God was doing, etc.—their murmurings delayed their progress in moving closer to God. Note that engaging in outer court "chatter" that distracts and/or causes us to engage in murmuring, complaining, and even gossip will hinder our prayers and keep us from moving forward.

As discussed in the last chapter, we must come to God through the Lord Jesus. However, this salvation experience is only the beginning of our faith walk. We must continue pursuing God and grow in our faith. Thus, we cannot be content to simply remain in the outer court of our relationship with God.

## The Pattern Applied to Prayer

There will be several levels of prayer through which we must move to reach the place of total surrender to God in prayer and intercession. We cannot pray as effectively in the outer court. We must pass through to maturity and into His presence by surrendering ourselves completely to God. In this place, His power fuels and transforms our prayers.

There are many people who enter the courts of the Lord, embrace religion, and never go deeper into His presence. However, God's desire is to lead us through the outer court into the Holy Place and then into the Most Holy Place—that inner sanctuary of intimate and pure communion with Him—the place where we experience His glory and are empowered to bring it back into the earthly realm.

## 1. The Brazen Altar

This is the first stage of our outer court experience in God's pattern of prayer and preparing to enter His presence. The brazen altar (or the altar of burnt offerings) is where we let go of our will and embrace everything the Lord wants to do in our lives.

The word altar in the Hebrew means 'a slaughter place'. In the Greek, it's called 'a place of sacrifice'. In other words, it is a place of death. It's the place where things of the flesh that hinder our walk with God are consumed by the fire of God. It's a place where we become a living sacrifice.

Paul states in Romans 12:1-2:

> I beseech you therefore, brethren, by the mercies of God, that you present your bodies a living sacrifice, holy, acceptable to God, which is your reasonable service. And do not be conformed to this world, but be transformed by the renewing of your mind, that you may prove what is that good and acceptable and perfect will of God.

Remember that sacrifice always comes before service. Many people are serving God in the Church—preaching, teaching, operating in the gifts, laying on of hands, speaking in tongues, leading praise and worship—but they haven't been to the brazen altar. They haven't stopped at the place of sacrifice and given everything to God. As a result, they are still controlled by their own will and desires. They are still in the outer court operating in the natural light.

Before we can operate in the Spirit realm and in prayer, we must stop at the altar and say, "God, whatever it is, I lay it down." Jesus is there with amazing grace to bring us through the fire.

In the first consecration service for Israel, Aaron performed the sacrifices according to the pattern God revealed to Moses. (See Leviticus 1-8) He followed God's pattern, and the glory of God was revealed to all the people. God consumed the sacrifice and atoned for Israel's sins.

The priests were instructed in Leviticus 6:12:

> *And the fire on the altar shall be kept burning on it; it shall not be put out. And the priest shall burn wood on it every morning, and lay the burnt offering in order on it; and he shall burn on it the fat of the peace offerings.*

From that day forward, wood—which represents humanity—kept the fire burning. In other words, God requires us to lay ourselves on the brazen altar every day and say, "Whatever doesn't please You, Lord, burn it up. Consume my will, my desires, my emotions, and anything else that doesn't line up with Your will. Not my will but Your will be done." We are the wood that keeps God's fire burning on the altar continuously.

There were four horns on the brazen altar of sacrifice, one on each corner. When a sacrificial animal was slaughtered for the atonement for sin, it was first tied to these four horns. Now, as I said before, there's purpose behind everything God does. As each person came to seek God, four steps were taken at the altar of brass, revealing four aspects of divine grace and God's love. These aspects hold a special significance even for us today.

The first aspect was _confession of sins_. In approaching the altar, the person's desire was for peace with God. To have that peace meant asking God for forgiveness with a heart of true repentance. For us, that's the first action when coming to God.

The second aspect was a _sacrifice had to be made for sin_. This sacrifice had to include the shedding of blood. The person bringing the sacrificial animal would lay their hand on its head, imputing or accrediting their sin to the animal so that it became guilty in their place. This is what Jesus did for us at Calvary on the cross. Jesus was the sacrificial Lamb that was slain with His blood shed to redeem mankind. So, in Jesus we have remission of sins, and our sins are blotted out forever. This understanding of Christ's sacrifice helps us comprehend the grace of God.

The third aspect was the _burning of the sacrifice_. At the brazen altar, the animal sacrificed on the altar was also burnt as an offering. Every burnt offering ascended to the heavens, literally going up in smoke. It was an exchange with Heaven to atone for sin. This represents the crucifixion of Jesus Christ on the cross. When Jesus died, sin was crucified and dealt with—it went up in smoke. Because of this, the sin nature can be exchanged for God's righteousness, His holiness.

The fourth aspect was the _consecration for service_. The priest would consecrate himself, by offering a sacrifice for his own sin. He could not go through the rituals otherwise. For us, this means that, before we enter the service of our God, we must be consecrated or sanctified for that purpose.

This is how we begin our journey into the presence of God. When we lay on the altar of sacrifice, we receive what we need to do His will (Kingdom service). We become resilient in prayer and strong in intercession. How? It is result of our flesh being consumed in the fire of God. Sin and the flesh can no longer hinder our prayers.

The songwriter, Elisha Hoffman, penned the following words in the song "Is Your All on the Altar?"[2]:

> You have longed for sweet peace,
> And for faith to increase,
> And have earnestly, fervently prayed;

---

[2] Elisha A. Hoffman, 1900. Public domain.

But you cannot have rest,
Or be perfectly blest,
Until all on the altar is laid.

*Refrain*
Is your all on the altar of sacrifice laid?
Your heart does the Spirit control?
You can only be blest,
And have peace and sweet rest,
As you yield Him your body and soul.

This first verse and chorus sum it up so well. Our very peace and rest along with answered prayer is tied to laying it all on the altar before God.

## 2. The Brazen Laver

Exodus 30:18-19 reads:

*"You shall also make a laver of bronze, with its base also of bronze, for washing. You shall put it between the tabernacle of meeting and the altar. And you shall put water in it, for Aaron and his sons shall wash their hands and their feet in water from it."*

The laver was a wash basin in the tabernacle that was filled with water for the washing of the hands and feet. This was significant. The priest had to wash his hands for service, and he had to wash his feet to guard his pathway and keep it pure before the Lord. God's instructions to Moses for the priests included the warning that, if they didn't wash, they would die.

Exodus 30:21 says:

> *"So they shall wash their hands and their feet, lest they die. And it shall be a statute forever to them—to him and his descendants throughout their generations."*

The brazen laver is the second stop on our journey and is symbolic of the need to wash ourselves with the Word of God. It is the place of purification and sanctification where the Word of God cleanses and prepares us to serve in our priestly function as intercessors. Our prayers now come from the Word—a pure place that is not tainted by our flesh and the world. It's imperative that we stop at the laver before we enter the Holy Place.

When a priest of the tabernacle approached the brazen laver, he saw his reflection in the water. There could be no mistake in how he looked. Similarly, when we go to the brazen laver in prayer, God shows us a true reflection of who we are. By coming to Him, we can see our natural reflection and get a glimpse of what we are becoming as He imparts the Word into our lives. A changed life begins when we look in the mirror and see ourselves. This is when we become conscious of becoming a true reflection of Him and doing what we need to according to the Word.

As we read in James 1:22-25:

*But be doers of the word, and not hearers only, deceiving yourselves. For if anyone is a hearer of the word and not a doer, he is like a man observing his natural face in a mirror; for he observes himself, goes away, and immediately forgets what kind of man he was. But he who looks into the perfect law of liberty and continues in it, and is not a forgetful hearer but a doer of the work, this one will be blessed in what he does.*

As was discussed back in Chapter 5, we must be doers of the Word, letting it transform us. We cannot only listen to God's Word, but we must also obey His Word as well. This is a command from God *"that He might sanctify and cleanse* [us] *with the washing of water by the word"*. (Ephesians 5:26) The Word acts as a cleansing agent in our lives.

The brazen laver represents something else just as vital in the believer's life today. It was made of bronze mirrors, which came from the women of Israel. Bronze symbolizes judgment. There is a cleansing character to the Word as we have learned, but the Word also judges the heart as we read about in Hebrews 4:12 where it says:

*For the word of God is living and powerful, and sharper than any two-edged sword, piercing even to the division of soul and spirit, and of joints and marrow, and is a discerner of the thoughts and intents of the heart.*

So, the brazen laver acts as a spiritual mirror in our lives and represents cleansing and judging by the Word of God.

John 15:3 (KJV) states:

*Now ye are clean through the Word which I have spoken unto you.*

Always remember the pattern: Jesus is the Way, the Way is the Word, and we can't have a successful, effective prayer life without the Word of God.

Once we have washed in the brazen laver, we cannot remain there. We are still in the outer court level of praying, so the only person we will be able to pray for is ourselves. Outer court prayer focuses on our wrongdoings, our limitations, our failures, what we need to overcome, and so on. We must move into the Holy Place.

## The Holy Place

In our journey thus far, we have come through the gate into the outer court and laid our all on the brazen altar. Then, Jesus became the Way for us to see our reflection, and we were purified and cleansed by the Word in the brazen laver. Now, we're at the door of the tabernacle. It's time to enter the Holy Place.

At this point, we have come into a place of serious intercession. When one becomes an intercessor, they stand in the gap on behalf of another person. In this place of intercession, we are walking with the Lord under a new anointing.

In the Holy Place, we are also operating in the supernatural light. God has not called us into this marvelous light for us to gaze at or be afraid of it, nor does He want us to go back to our comfort zone in the outer court of natural light. Instead, there's a divine purpose for us in this place where God gives us the grace to do what He's called us to do. He lights our way, bringing revelation to fulfill His will.

### 1. The Table of Shewbread

The table of shewbread was placed on the north or right side of the tabernacle where it faced the candlestick on the opposite side of the room. Twelve unleavened loaves of bread made of fine wheat flour and representing the twelve tribes of Israel were placed upon the table and arranged in two rows or piles of six. (Exodus 40:22-23, Leviticus 24:5-6)

Only the priests could enter the Holy Place as representatives of the people to perform daily rituals of worship. Every seven days on the Sabbath, they had to replace the shewbread with fresh loaves. The old shewbread was removed to be eaten by the priests exclusively and in a sacred place. (Leviticus 24:8-9)

The priests were also to put some pure frankincense on each row of bread to serve as a representative offering, a special gift presented to the Lord. Every Sabbath day when this bread was laid out fresh before the Lord, it was done as a gift from the Israelites as an ongoing expression of the eternal covenant. (Leviticus 24:7-8)

For us today, the shewbread holds a lot of significance. First, it represents the eternal covenant between God and His people. As believers, we are the people of God. Secondly, Jesus—the One who made a way for us to become the children of God—is the Bread of Life. As our High Priest, He has mediated for us a better covenant with God the Father. (Hebrews 8:6) Also, bread is always a type or symbol of strength. (Psalms 104:15) As such, the bread is symbolic of the life and strength that is ours in Christ Jesus along with the New Covenant we have with the Father.

So, as an intercessor we must eat of Christ to become like Him and be prepared to battle in the heavenly realm through our prayers. We must digest the Word regularly to receive strength and maintain a transformed lifestyle.

In Psalms 34:8-10, it says:

*Oh, taste and see that the Lord is good; blessed is the man who trusts in Him! Oh, fear the Lord, you His saints! There is no want to those who fear Him. The young lions lack and suffer hunger; but those who seek the Lord shall not lack any good thing.*

As the saints, we have been made *"priests to our God"* (Revelation 5:10). The Bread of Life will sustain us in life and prayer as part of our New Covenant promise with God.

## 2. The Golden Candlestick (Menorah)

When the priest walked through the first veil into the Holy Place, he stepped into a dim, enclosed space. Heavy curtains kept natural, outdoor light from penetrating. The golden candlestick or lampstand provided the only light in the Holy Place. It stood on the south or left side of the Holy place, directly opposite the table of shewbread.

The candlestick was made of pure gold. The different parts were of "beaten" work hammered out of sheets. It had a central stem, which represented God, with six branches (three on each side), which represented man. (Exodus 37:17-18)

The purpose of the golden candlestick was for light and illumination day and night. Therefore, it symbolizes divine understanding and the illumination of the Word, the next level of insight and revelation where Word and Spirit are one.

## 3. The Oil

It was the priest's task to keep the Menorah filled with oil. The priest also had to keep the wick of the candles trimmed. Unless the burnt part of the wick was removed, smoke would be mixed with light in the Holy Place and create an impure atmosphere. Nothing was to be unholy in the Holy Place.

When we look at the process used to make the olive oil used in the Menorah, it speaks strongly of the separation or threshing process. Basically, as olives grow to maturity, the early fruit falls to the ground. During harvest time, the trees are beaten with long sticks to yield the rest of the crop. Then, all the olives are gathered off the ground. In Bible days, they pressed out the oil either by crushing the olives in a vat-like hollow stone with large stones or by treading upon them with their feet.

Let me stop here and say, there is no anointing without the process of beating and pressing. When we go through trials and testing, the oil of anointing will continue to flow in our lives as we submit to the process God is using to extract that which is holy.

In the Old Testament, the ordinance of anointing with oil was the most common and significant ceremony. The tabernacle was anointed, the priests were anointed, the prophets were anointed, the kings were anointed, and the sick were anointed. It was a special symbol of the Holy Ghost and the dedication of the person called to His service. Therefore, this pure oil used in the Menorah symbolizes the anointing of the Holy Spirit.

By the time we reach the Holy Place in prayer, we should be operating consistently in the newness of God. Old things are passed away—having been separated or threshed out—and all things have become new. For this reason, our "wicks" (lives) must be trimmed daily so that there will be no residue of what used to be.

## 4. The Golden Altar

The golden altar or altar of incense was overlaid with pure gold. It occupied the middle space just in front of the inner veil separating the Holy Place from the Holy of Holies. (Exodus 30:1-6) The purpose of the golden altar was threefold: prayer, intercession, and worship, and its fire was never supposed to go out.

Every morning and evening, the priests would burn a special incense there. The incense also required special preparation, for the priests had to crush the spices into a powder and then blend them together perfectly in equal proportions. When they placed that incense on the live coals, a beautiful, fragrant, white smoke would rise up from the altar. The compound that produced this beautiful fragrance was comprised of four different ingredients: stacte, onycha, galbanum, and frankincense. (Exodus 30:34)

Let's examine these four ingredients a little more...

STACTE comes from the Hebrew word *nataph,* which means 'to drop' or 'to ooze'. It is a gum-resin that oozes spontaneously from the tree that contains it.

True worshipers will spontaneously respond to the goodness of our God. As we are in prayer and daily digesting the Word, our hearts will "ooze" with gratitude for His lovingkindness.

ONYCHA comes from the Hebrew word *shecheleth*, meaning 'to roar; as a lion'. It's an ingredient derived from mollusks found in the depths of the Red Sea. The onycha emits a peculiar odor when burned.

Just as the mollusk is found in the depths of the sea, it exemplifies real worship that "roars" from an otherwise untapped depth within our hearts. It is also a picture of the openness and honesty that God desires in our worship. We cannot pretend to worship or choose to worship in our own way without paying the consequences for our actions. God knows whether or not we are truly expressing our hearts to Him or just going through the motions.

GALBANUM is derived from the Hebrew word *chelbnah*, which is a gum-resin. It is the third ingredient in the perfume of worship. The gum-resin occurs in small, round, semi-translucent "tears" or in brownish-yellow masses. It has a pleasant aromatic odor but a bitter taste.

The semi-translucent tears and bitter taste represent a picture of the brokenness that God yearns for in our worship. He desires that we come into His presence revealing the depth of a broken and contrite heart. This means that our hearts are repentant, and we approach God from a place of willing and humble obedience.

FRANKINCENSE is the same as the Hebrew word *lebonah*, which means 'whiteness'. It is a white substance obtained by wounding the Boswellia sacra tree and then removing the sap that bleeds out. That sap is then dried.

Frankincense represents the holiness that God alone brings to our worship. The purity of His holiness mingles with the sacrifices of our broken, contrite hearts and becomes a sweet-smelling fragrance before the throne of God as our worship ascends unto Him.

One of the noblest qualities about the golden altar was that it was positioned in the center of the room, so it sat in the heart of the holy place. This correlates to intercession touching the heart of God.

The golden altar of incense represents a place of worship and total surrender with the incense being symbolic of our prayers and intercession. Incense (prayer) in the Holy Place is the only element capable of ushering us into the divine presence of God.

Interestingly, the fires of both the golden altar in the Holy Place and the brazen altar in the outer court were first lit by God and then kept burning continuously.

"After both altars were lit supernaturally, the priests kept the fires burning continually, taking coals off the brazen altar daily and using them to keep the fire kindled at the golden altar, representing that the fire in our worship, intercession and prayer—though it is rekindled by our ongoing sacrifice—must come directly from God."[i]

As we have learned, the fire on the golden altar—our prayers, intercession, and worship—are to never cease. We are to offer this incense continuously and sacrificially to the Lord.

## Before We Enter

Before we enter the Holy of Holies, I must stop here and explain what God requires of us before we enter this sacred and intimate space.

### 1. Sacrifice

The children of Israel brought their burnt offerings, which were unblemished bulls, sheep, goats, pigeons, or turtledoves. These unblemished animals symbolized the moral perfection demanded by a holy God and the perfect sacrifice that was to come, Jesus Christ. The purpose for these offerings was to make an atonement for sin.

We are to sacrificially lay our lives down—our thoughts, feelings, agendas, ideas, desires, etc.—on the altar so that we can enter the Holy of Holies. Because Jesus was made sin for us, we can boldly enter through His righteousness and perfection which are now ours. We don't become holy in our own strength but are made holy through our surrender to Jesus as our Lord and Savior.

## 2. Genuine Repentance

God requires more than sacrifice though. He also asks His children to have an attitude of repentance. To repent means to feel remorse over one's sin or faults in order to change one's life and do better. In other words, there must be an inward change as the prerequisite to living a transformed life. God requires genuine repentance in coming before Him in the Most Holy Place.

## 3. Internal Fire

We need a fire deep within our spirits and in our hearts to bring us into the true worship of our God. Coal that has already been burned is unsightly since it has no fire and is no longer of any use. God is not interested in dead coals. Instead, He wants a people who are continuously on fire for Him.

## 4. Reverence and Awe

God is so deserving of all our adoration and worship. Thus, He wants us to have an attitude of true reverence and awe towards Him. This posture pleases Him immensely. This is characteristic of true worship, and it sends up a sweet aroma that truly delights Him.

Are you ready to lay your all on the altar before your God? Have you truly repented and accepted the righteousness that is yours? Are you genuinely on fire for Him, ready to follow and obey? How is your attitude toward Him? Is it one that will please Him?

It is important to examine these questions honestly as you prepare to enter the Holy of Holies, that Most Holy Place of worship before our God.

# The Most Holy Place

The Most Holy Place was the inner sanctuary of the tabernacle located behind the veil that separated it from the Holy Place. In it, the Ark of the Covenant or the Ark of the Testimony was placed. Inside the Ark, the following items were kept:

- *The Ten Commandments* – As given to Moses, these stone tablets represented God's perfect law and commandments. (Exodus 24:12)

- *A gold jar containing miraculously preserved manna* – This represented God's provision. (Exodus 16:33-34)

- *Aaron's rod that budded* – This was a reminder that God would not tolerate rebellion. (Numbers 17:8-10)

The Ark was overlaid with pure gold, inside and out. The Ark's cover was called the mercy seat or the seat of atonement, and it was made of pure gold. On top of it, two cherubim faced each other, looking down upon the mercy seat with their wings thrust forward in a brooding attitude as if protecting it. (Exodus 25:10-21)

In the space above the mercy seat between where the golden cherubim hovered, God told Moses He would meet him there to talk with him. Here, He would give Moses commands for the people of Israel to follow. (Exodus 25:22)

No unclean or sinful man could go before the mercy seat or approach the holiness of the all-holy God, not even the anointed high priest. If he went before it for his own pleasure or without the required blood sacrifice, he would subject himself to immediate death. Going behind the veil into the inner sanctuary required intentional steps of preparation.

Jehovah manifested His presence in a cloud, which was known as the Shekinah. Shekinah is a Hebrew name that means 'dwelling'. The Shekinah was the glory of the Lord—His presence—that covered and inhabited the tabernacle.

187

The Holy of Holies is a place where we have eternal communion with God. When we come to Him as we ought—sacrificially, having repented and been made clean, on fire for Him, with the right attitude and a heart of true worship—He will meet us in this sacred space. Once we enter into His presence, it is a time to listen, for this is the time when God speaks and reveals mysteries, provides answers to prayer, and gives instructions, just as He did for Moses.

When we're in the Holy of Holies, we are in another realm entirely. We are not aware of our physical surroundings. We're cut off from the world and in another dimension where we are in the presence of the Most Holy God. We experience His love, power, and glory. Our heart and His heart are joined together—spirit to Spirit.

I believe that most Christians have not had a "behind the veil" experience. They think they have, but they have no idea what it even means. Most believers have mistaken "behind the veil" experiences as being those times when they were touched deeply during a high point in a service or when they were slain in the Spirit during worship. Although these things can be part of the experience, it does not constitute the fullness of this intimate, spiritual encounter with God. Why? Going behind the veil is not a one-time event or experience. It's a lifestyle.

# CHAPTER TEN

## Worshiping Him

In the book of Genesis, we find an example of a "first mention principle" as it is sometimes referred to. This is when a biblical principle is referenced for the first time, and it establishes the original intent of God within the context of its text. As a principle, it lays the foundation for a truth that will not change later. In other words, no matter the situation, circumstance, time period, culture, etc., that truth applies and is constant. It is the truth about the matter from Genesis through Revelation.

The first mention principle of worship is found in Genesis 22:5, which reads:

> *And Abraham said to his young men, "Stay here with the donkey; the lad and I will go yonder and worship, and we will come back to you."*

The meaning of worship in this text speaks of lowering oneself in humility and adoration to God. It also means to bow down and yield to Him. When we offer Him adoration, we are honoring and glorifying Him. When we worship Him in humility, we are worshiping in humbleness, meekness, submission, obedience, and lowliness of mind. This was and is God's intent for worship. This principle for worship is unchanging.

Several Old Testament Scriptures exhort us to worship no other god but the Lord, and that if you do, you shall surely perish. This also sets forth a principle or foundation for the focus of our worship.

Could this be one of the problems we are seeing in many of our churches today? Could it be that many Christians have become so caught up with the things of this world—worshiping other gods—that they have no space left for God?

The Word commands us in Psalms 29:2 to:

*Give unto the Lord the glory due His name; Worship the Lord in the beauty of holiness.*

We are to ascribe worth to God through our speech and conduct and especially our worship. In worship, we address God directly, expressing reverence for His nature, character, attributes, and power, in addition to acknowledging and esteeming Him for all that He has done, is doing, and will do for us.

## Worshiping from the Heart

The foremost reason for worship is to minister unto the Lord with a sincere heart. In my journey, I have learned one main thing... If it's not real, it's just entertainment with no power and no anointing. We were created to worship, but it *has* to be real.

What comes from the heart will reach the heart of God. Therefore, only one type of worshiper will get God's attention and that is a true worshiper. Their worship pleases God because it comes from an obedient heart. The omniscient, all-knowing God seeks us to worship Him from the heart, for He *loves* the heart of a true worshiper!

God has tolerated our ignorance and disobedience long enough when it comes to worship. He is a merciful God, but the time has come for us to ascribe to Him the true worship that He desires and is due His name. No longer should worship leaders be satisfied pushing emotional buttons to ignite a response from a crowd during a worship service. No longer should believers go through the motions for show and in pride. No longer should Christians give their worship half-heartedly to the Lord. It doesn't matter where we worship. It matters *how* we worship and *who* we worship.

Jesus says in Matthew 15:8-9a:

*"These people draw near to Me with their mouth, and honor Me with their lips, but their heart is far from Me, and in vain they worship Me..."*

Not being a true worshiper of God is serious indeed. In fact, it is worship that is *"in vain"* as verse 9 reads. This means it serves no purpose. When you think about that in terms of relationship with God...there isn't one.

A true worshiper is one who worships Him in spirit and in truth. This type of worship is from the depths of our inward parts, a place where we completely abandon ourselves before Him. It's not about how well we sing or how well we play an instrument. Instead, it's all about how we live our lives, especially when no one is watching.

Only one type of worshiper gets God's attention and that is a true worshiper. True worshipers seek God's Word and His Spirit in all things, whereas counterfeits only use God for what they can get out of Him. A true worshiper honors God.

## Old Testament Worship

We can learn a lot about worship through the Old Testament, particularly in the study of the Psalms. The Psalms are a collection of poems, songs, prayers, and prophetic utterances. They encompass expressions of contrition, supplication, thanksgiving, and adoration or praise.

The Book of Psalms or the *Tehillim* in Hebrew means 'Book of Praises'. When we come to the New Testament, we find that the Psalms are quoted or referenced more often than any other part of the Old Testament.

Let's look at a couple of true worshipers who contributed to the composition of the Psalms.

## 1. David

David was the youngest son of the eight sons of Jesse. He was a shepherd boy who matured into a mighty warrior. Later in life, he became the second and greatest king of Israel. As an eloquent poet and talented musician, he composed 73 of the 150 Psalms in the Bible.

David was considered a man after God's own heart. Why? It is because he pursued God wholeheartedly. He was genuine in faith and devotion, willing to do what God asked Him to do. (Acts 13:22)

As *"the sweet psalmist of Israel"* (2 Samuel 23:1), David expressed many songs of praise and adoration towards God. David was a true worshiper.

As a prophet, David was moved by the Holy Spirit to set forth many glorious truths in the Psalms that relate to Christ as our Savior and Messiah. (Acts 2:29-31) These prophetic songs (psalms) were also sung and confessed through worship.

In studying the life of David and the Psalms, we can learn a great deal about music used in worship. For example, a variety of instruments were played, and there were different types of songs that were sung unto the Lord. I can imagine that the music that accompanied the Psalms was beautiful. One thing is sure, music occupied an important place in the life of the Jewish people, especially in their worship of God.

David loved music so much that he set up a music ministry in the tabernacle. He appointed musicians and singers to minister to the Lord day and night. David possessed a heart for true worship.

## 2. Asaph

Asaph was the chief worship leader appointed by David to serve in the tabernacle until the temple was completed. He penned Psalms 50, 73-83. David established the tradition of delivering psalms to Asaph for the tabernacle singers to sing.

In 1 Chronicles 16:7, we read:

> *On that day David first delivered this psalm into the hand of Asaph and his brethren, to thank the Lord:*

The name Asaph means 'to gather or collect'. The word thank in Hebrew is *yadah*, includes the definition of 'to praise and give thanks' and especially 'to revere or worship' through the extending of the hands.

Just like Asaph, worship leaders have an anointing to "gather" the people of God into His presence so that they can experience God's glory through praise and worship. As true worshipers, when we give thanks, praise, and worship to our God, there is usually some type of external expression. It could be the lifting of the hands, clapping, bowing down, or bowing the head.

Whatever the case, an outward extension of our worship before the Lord tells God, "I am worshiping You."

Now, Asaph was the father of the clan of temple musicians who served in the temple. Not only was he a worship leader, but he also played instruments. Serving with Him were Heman and Jeduthun, along with their sons and brothers as we read about in 2 Chronicles 5:12:

> *and the Levites who were the singers, all those of Asaph and Heman and Jeduthun, with their sons and their brethren, stood at the east end of the altar, clothed in white linen, having cymbals, stringed instruments and harps, and with them one hundred and twenty priests sounding with trumpets—*

As the singers would sing, 2 Chronicles 5:13-14 tells us that:

> *indeed, it came to pass, when the trumpeters and singers were as one, to make one sound to be heard in praising and thanking the Lord, and when they lifted up their voice with the trumpets and cymbals and instruments of music, and praised the Lord saying: "For He is good, for His mercy endures forever," that the house, the house of the Lord, was filled with a cloud, so that the priests could not continue ministering because of the cloud; for the glory of the Lord filled the house of God.*

Notice that this Scripture says that the singers were as one. That meant they were in unity one with another. God is not the author of confusion. Therefore, if worship leaders, singers, or any musician perform to draw attention to themselves and not to God, they need to reevaluate their reasons for being part of the worship team.

Asaph was also a prophetic seer who sung prophetically. A prophetic seer is one who sees into the Spirit realm and prophesies what is seen—in word, song, or with a musical instrument. As a seer, Asaph delivered prophetic messages under God's Spirit.

In addition to Asaph's psalms, other prophetic declarations in the Book of Psalms include, Psalms 2, 16, 22, 40, 45, 68, 69, 72, 87, 97, 110, 118.

I truly believe that a prophetic singer is an intercessor or seer. We need these prophetic musicians who flow in the realm of the Holy Spirit, able to generate spontaneous lyrics and music. We do not see this very much in our modern-day churches.

Nevertheless, God is doing a new thing. As in the days of the Israelites in the desert, we all need to follow the cloud—the glory and presence of God. There is a need for our praise and worship to be taken to another dimension.

When true praise and worship are released, it creates an atmosphere for the supernatural. Many people today need to encounter restoration in their relationships, health, or emotions.

Some have been hurt, molested, taken advantage of, stolen from, or their lives have been destroyed in some other way. Others are plagued by demonic forces. So, in this type of atmosphere, they can be restored because the praise and worship provide an atmosphere for miracles, healing, and deliverance.

When anointed pastors, worship leaders, psalmists, singers, minstrels, worship teams, and musicians come together in unity and a right spirit before the Lord, the glory of God *will* appear, and the people will be made whole.

## New Testament Worship

In the New Testament, the meaning of worship is 'to crouch, prostrate oneself in homage, to do reverence to, adore'. This is the essence of heavenly worship lifted up and directed towards our God. We are to humble ourselves (bow down), pay homage, revere, and give our adoration to Him.

In addition, Philippians 3:3 says:

*For we are the circumcision, who worship God in the Spirit, rejoice in Christ Jesus, and have no confidence in the flesh,*

Circumcision means 'to cut'. As believers redeemed through Christ, our sins have been cut out of us. Jesus' sacrifice on the cross made a way for us to deal with the flesh, so that we can have fellowship with God. Worship in the Spirit is devoid of the flesh and its influence. It is the result of spiritual circumcision.

## 1. The Woman of Samaria

Every worshiper and worship leader should know John 4:23 by heart. Jesus Himself spoke these words to a woman in Samaria. Jesus is still speaking these words to us today.

> *"But the hour is coming, and now is, when the true worshipers will worship the Father in Spirit and truth; for the Father is seeking such to worship Him."*

In this Scripture, there is a gauge that measures our motives. It is to the Father that we direct our worship (who), we worship Him in spirit and in truth (how), and we offer that which has been defined by God as right and holy (what). This determines our true worship.

As I was studying the context of this passage (see John 4:1-26), I noticed that the words worship, worshiped, and worshipers are mentioned eight times combined. When we study the Bible and notice a reoccurring word, that word is considered to be the main point the speaker is trying to convey. Jesus was making it very clear in this passage the importance of worship and our role in worshiping the Father.

Next, I meditated on the number eight, which represents a new beginning. Biblically, it also stands for resurrection, a reflection of a new order or creation and man's true "born-again" experience.

In the story, Jesus had a "must need" to go to Samaria so that a certain woman could receive a new order of life and have a born-again experience. Because of His omniscience, He sat waiting for her arrival at Jacob's well.

The Samaritan woman arrived on schedule, and Jesus asked her for a drink. She couldn't believe that a Jew would ask her for a drink. Since Samaritans were half-Jewish mixed with the Assyrians, the Jews had no dealings with them because they considered them unclean.

Jesus engaged her in a conversation saying, *"If you knew the gift of God and who it is who says to you 'Give Me a drink,' you would have asked Him, and He would have given you living water."* (John 4:10) Intrigued, she made an inquiry of His greatness above Jacob who had provided the well and questioned how He could draw water with no vessel to do so.

In John 4:13-14, Jesus responded:

*"Whoever drinks of this water will thirst again, but whoever drinks of the water that I shall give him will never thirst. But the water that I shall give him will become in him a fountain of water springing up into everlasting life."*

Instantly, He had her undivided attention. He had brought her to a point of desiring this water, so He could minister to her need. He gently confronted her about her living with a man who was not her husband but did not condemn her for being immoral. This led her to perceive that He was a prophet because He told her all about her lifestyle without having met her before.

In her quest to know more about this prophet, she began talking about worshiping on Mt. Gerizim. This was where the Samaritans built a temple as a rival place of worship because they were not allowed to worship in Jerusalem.

Now we see the full context of John 4:23 in Jesus' response, starting in verse 21 and ending in verse 24:

> ..."Woman, believe Me, the hour is coming when you will neither on this mountain, nor in Jerusalem, worship the Father. You worship what you do not know; we know what we worship, for salvation is of the Jews. But the hour is coming, and now is, when the true worshipers will worship the Father in spirit and truth, for the Father is seeking such to worship Him. God is Spirit, and those who worship Him must worship in spirit and truth."

The Samaritan woman recognized the reality and revelation of the truth as she experienced the Living Water—Jesus. This truth caused her to spread the good news to her city. Many Samaritans came to Jesus and believed in Him because of her testimony.

What we learn from this story and the context of Jesus' command to worship the Father in spirit and in truth is that it starts with a relationship with our Savior. We must partake of the Living Water, seeking Jesus as our way to the Father. New Testament worship is about relationship—an intimacy of knowing our God and exalting Him for who He is.

As we develop our relationship of worship with the Father, our cry should be, "Father, please change me continually. I want to be a true worshiper. I want to worship You in the life of the Spirit and according to Your Word."

### 2. The Alabaster Box

Worshiping the Father in spirit and in truth requires other things from us as we learn through the anointing of Jesus at Bethany...

While Simon, the leper, and Jesus were eating together, Mary of Bethany brought an alabaster box full of precious ointment and poured it on His head and used it to anoint His feet, wiping them with her hair. (Mark 14:3-9, John 12:1-3) This occurred just before the Last Supper when the priests and the scribes were plotting to put Jesus to death.

This precious ointment was very valuable and worth a full year's wages. In anointing Jesus with it, she was giving everything she had as she lavished it on Him.

If we are true worshipers, there will be a desire in our hearts to give to God in some way or another. We will want to give our time, our devotion, our money, our everything. We will not come empty handed, for giving is a sign of true worship.

We also learn that this woman broke the alabaster box before anointing Jesus. She had to break it, for that was the only way the perfumed ointment could flow out. In like manner, some of us keep our emotions stored up and contained as if in an alabaster box. We need to break the protective walls that surround our feelings so that we can let them flow out and lavish them on the Lord. True worshipers are completely open and "broken" before the Lord.

## Jesus' Victory Over Temptation

After Jesus was baptized in water, He was led by the Spirit into the wilderness to be tempted by the devil for forty days and forty nights. Jesus fasted during this time and was very hungry afterwards. In Matthew 4:3, we read that the tempter came to Him and said:

> *"If You are the Son of God, command that these stones become bread."*

Jesus answered in Matthew 4:4, saying:

*"It is written, 'Man shall not live by bread alone, but by every word that proceeds from the mouth of God.'"*

The passage goes on in verses 5-6:

*Then the devil took Him up into the holy city, set Him on the pinnacle of the temple, and said to Him, "If You are the Son of God, throw Yourself down. For it is written: 'He shall give His angels charge over you,' and, 'In their hands they shall bear you up, lest you dash your foot against a stone.'"*

Jesus' response to Satan in verse 7 was:

*"It is written again, 'You shall not tempt the Lord your God.'"*

The devil was not done with the Lord. He took Him up onto a high mountain to show Him all the kingdoms of the world, offering them in all their glory to Jesus for a price as we read about in verse 9:

*"All these things I will give You if You will fall down and worship me."*

Satan desires to receive worship that only belongs to God. Before he fell, the Bible says, he was *"the anointed cherub who covers"* (Ezekiel 28:14) which indicates his high office of authority with the responsibility to protect and cover the holy mountain of God. Lucifer had been the guardian of God's throne, the one responsible for the atmosphere of worship that continually surrounds the throne of God. But when rebellion was found in him, Satan declared that he would ascend and become like the Most High God. (Isaiah 14:13-14) He is still trying to deceive men and women into worshiping him as though he was God.

In Matthew 4:10, we see Jesus' response to this temptation:

*"Away with you, Satan! For it is written, 'You shall worship the Lord your God, and Him only you shall serve.'"*

In declaring the imperative to worship God and Him only, Jesus' response also enlightens our understanding to know that whomever we worship, that's whom we will serve. Whatever we've made into an idol in our lives will become our master. It is inevitable that we serve whomever or whatever we worship.

Paul confirms this fact in Romans 6:16:

*Do you not know that to whom you present yourselves slaves to obey, you are that one's slaves whom you obey, whether of sin leading to death, or of obedience leading to righteousness?*

Has there been a time when the devil has come to tempt you? What did you do? Did you give in, or did you resist him with the Word?

I encourage you today to follow the example of Jesus and speak His words in response to the enemy. Tell Satan that you worship the Lord your God, and Him only will you serve!

## Hindrances to Worship

The flesh will hinder our praise and worship along with our prayers and intercession. As we are maturing in our relationship with God through our worship, we must be aware of the hindrances of the flesh that could stifle our spiritual growth and negatively impact our fellowship with the Lord, including our worship. I will name a few.

### 1. Sin

The presence of sin (or iniquity) in our lives can hinder our worship. Iniquity is defined as a deep-seated ill-will, hatred, or wickedness that opposes God's standard of righteousness. Any offering we make to the Lord—worship, prayers, etc.—are hampered if iniquity is present.

The psalmist in Psalm 66:18 (KJV) cried:

*If I regard iniquity in my heart, the Lord will not hear me:*

Isaiah 59:2 declares:

> But your iniquities have separated you from your God;
> and your sins have hidden His face from you, so that He
> will not hear.

While the Scriptures do not teach that we must be sinless to enter into worship, they are clear that we must be willing to repent of known sin in order to walk in fellowship with God. Repentance must become a lifestyle for the believer so that we can be continually cleansed from sin as we are convicted by the Holy Spirit.

## 2. Distractions

When Jesus spent time with Mary and Martha, He observed two aspects of the Christian life. One was that of service and the other was one of worship. Both were (are) good, but one was (is) better.

As we read in Luke 10:40-42:

> But Martha was distracted with much serving, and she
> approached Him and said, "Lord, do You not care that my
> sister has left me to serve alone? Therefore tell her to
> help me."

*And Jesus answered and said to her, "Martha, Martha, you are worried and troubled about many things. But one thing is needed, and Mary has chosen that good part, which will not be taken away from her."*

Martha was unable to worship because she was distracted by service. This kept her from sitting at the feet of Jesus and expressing her devotion to Him.

On the other hand, Mary chose to feast on the words of Jesus. She basked in the presence of God. Jesus made it known that Mary had chosen the better path, that of worship.

I have noticed this same problem amongst believers today. Many are so busy serving, they neglect to take the time to truly worship. So many of us are consumed with "doing life" that we forget to worship Him. We have become slaves to our schedules and personal pursuits—running here and there, tied up in the hustle and bustle of life—all to the point that we don't even feel like taking time to be in the Lord's presence. In this process, we miss out on the most wonderful opportunity of our lives.

It takes time to enter into God's presence. The biggest joy of our lives should be taking time out to be with Him, to sit at His feet and be blessed. Pursuing the presence of God should be our priority.

### 3. Unforgiveness

We cannot worship God and be angry or bitter at other Christians.

John put it best in 1 John 4:20 (AMPC):

*If anyone says, I love God, and hates (detests, abominates) his brother [in Christ], he is a liar; for he who does not love his brother, whom he has seen, cannot love God, Whom he has not seen.*

Jesus said in Matthew 5:23-24:

*"Therefore if you bring your gift to the altar, and there remember that your brother has something against you, leave your gift there before the altar, and go your way. First be reconciled to your brother, and then come and offer your gift."*

Basically, if we have a problem with others and are not operating in forgiveness, we must make that right before we come and try to pretend that we love God.

### 4. Ignorance

Biblical ignorance keeps people from worshiping God in spirit and in truth. We can't worship someone we don't know, and we can't know God unless we are a student of His Word.

## 5. Condemnation

This hindrance shows up when we feel that we are unworthy to come to God because of bad behavior and our past. When people sin, there's a tendency to run *from* God rather than run *to* God. Yet, because of the work of the cross, our sins have been forgiven. By faith, we need to accept and receive His forgiveness and worship Him despite the sin from our past.

## 6. Fear

One specific fear that can hinder us from giving our everything in worship is the fear of what people might think or say. Internally, we are held back with thoughts such as "What will my friends think if I fall prostrate on the floor or raise my hands? Will I look dumb or hypocritical?" These questions and others like it are all rooted in the fear of man and ultimately in the spirit of pride.

John 12:42-43 says:

> *Nevertheless even among the rulers many believed in Him, but because of the Pharisees they did not confess Him, lest they should be put out of the synagogue; for they loved the praise of men more than the praise of God.*

So, don't be concerned with what others think. The real question is, "What does God think?" His opinion is the only one that matters.

### 7. Feelings

Our emotions play a big part in worship, but honestly, sometimes we just don't feel like it. This is a struggle, and ultimately, we must learn to worship God anyway no matter how we may feel. It's called a sacrifice of praise.

As Jesus said in Matthew 26:41:

> "Watch and pray, lest you enter into temptation. The spirit indeed is willing, but the flesh is weak."

# Our Bridegroom is coming!

In my study of the Word, I discovered that the bride or wife of Christ is not the New Testament Church, one's church denomination, Israel, the 144,000 Jews, or the tribulation saints. It is unscriptural to speak of any one company of redeemed as being the exclusive bride of Christ. No, the collective bride of Christ includes everyone who lives under the New Covenant and all those who reside in the holy city at the end of the age.

Revelation 21:9-10 (NLT) says:

> Then one of the seven angels who held the seven bowls containing the seven last plagues came and said to me, "Come with me! I will show you the bride, the wife of the Lamb." So he took me in the Spirit to a great, high

*mountain, and he showed me the holy city, Jerusalem, descending out of heaven from God.*

If the holy city—the New Jerusalem—is the bride, then all who go to live in the holy city make up the bride. Therefore, all who are married to Christ under the terms of the New Covenant are citizens of Heaven. As believers, we have the hope and assurance of going to live in the New Jerusalem as a part of the bride of Christ and residents of the heavenly city.

## 1. We must be ready!

Matthew 25:10 states:

*And while they went to buy, the bridegroom came, and those who were ready went in with him to the wedding; and the door was shut.*

Our Bridegroom, Jesus Christ, is coming for us. However, we, the Church, must prepare ourselves for His return. We must be ready, watchful, and waiting, for we do not know the day nor the hour of His coming. (Matthew 25:13)

The Lord has waited a long time for us to prepare ourselves for the glad day of His return. He longs for each of His children to become true worshipers with hearts of worship and adoration for Him and Him only.

- Do you understand the urgency of the command to be ready for His return?

- Do you consider yourself as blessed to be one of His beloved?

- Are you acting as His bride—excited and expectant—earnestly preparing for the Bridegroom's arrival?

The life of the believer is about having an intimate relationship with the Lord. It is pursuing the heart of the Father, following His Son, and moving by the Spirit. It is all about living as true worshipers of the Most High God.

In light of the magnitude of what is to come on that glorious day, how insignificant are all the cares, trials, and tribulations we are enduring or will endure. How small they seem when our eyes are turned with expectancy toward Him coming in the clouds.

## 2. Preparation is now!

The Lord is sanctifying and cleansing the Church—His bride—with the washing of water by His Word that He *"might present it to himself a glorious church, not having spot, or wrinkle, or any such thing; but that it should be holy and without blemish."* (Ephesians 5:26-27, KJV)

The Lord's Church is made up of everyone who is committed to becoming His glorious bride, completely free from all sin. Having been partakers of His divine nature and having escaped the corruption that is in the world through lust, this is the beautiful bride the Lord is looking for.

Those who are on this path understand the need to prepare and make themselves ready for Christ's return. They are the ones who love Jesus and follow Him. They are the ones who ache with longing to be in His presence, who hunger and thirst after Him. They are the ones who have decided to serve Jesus with all their heart. They are the ones whom Jesus has cleansed and purified. They are those who will shine with a brightness, a purity, and a holiness just as He who called them is holy. They are the ones who are intimate with Him in relationship and through their worship. They ARE the glorious Church without spot or wrinkle.

Every opportunity that we have should be in preparing ourselves for the Bridegroom—Jesus. We are to make ourselves ready while living righteously here on earth. BLESSED are we who are called according to His purpose...to be made into His bride.

As we read in Revelation 19:9:

*Then he said to me, "Write: 'Blessed are those who are called to the marriage supper of the Lamb!'" And he said to me, "These are the true sayings of God."*

Therefore, may our prayer always be, "Even so, come, Lord Jesus! Come quickly!"

Yet, as Matthew 22:14 says:

*"For many are called, but few are chosen."*

Countless invitations have been sent out, but many choose not to answer. Just because people attend church services and Bible studies, does not mean that they are chosen. If there is no change in their lives, if they simply are going through the motions of Christian living, and if they are not preparing themselves as the bride of Christ, they are in danger of hearing those fearful words, *"I do not know you"* as we read about in Matthew 25:12.

We should be excited to prepare for the Lord's coming! Our anticipation should have us joyfully pursuing an intimate relationship with our God. In the natural, when a couple becomes engaged, the next step is preparation. There is an intense love for one another and a longing to be united forever. The expectation of what is to come drives the relationship and, hopefully, doing what it takes to prepare for that next step.

How much more should we prepare ourselves for our Bridegroom?

There should be an intense love for Him, one that motivates our obedience to Him. There should be a longing to be united with Him. Whatever it takes, as the bride of Christ, our desire is to do anything and everything—paying any cost—in order to be worthy of Him and to be with Him.

Some questions for you are:

- Does the love you have for God inspire you to want to obey Him in all things?
- Do you allow Him to speak to you and instruct you?
- Is there any intimacy between you and the Lord?
- Are you preparing yourself for your Bridegroom? How?

You may ask yourself, "How can I have intimacy with someone I can't see?" Many have struggled with this question and the questions above. Many people want to be able to discern His voice and experience that type of love, but they haven't "felt" the intensity that has them falling over in their devotion and excitement.

To begin with, an intimate relationship with the Lord takes intentionality on your part. God will always do His part, but you will have to make room to receive all that He has for you. My suggestion is to take some quiet time with the Lord by taking the following steps:

**Step 1 –** *Surrender your heart totally to Him.* Just as you would in the natural if you were deeply in love, give yourself completely to the Lord. This was your choice when you were born again, and it must continue to be your daily choice moving forward in your relationship.

**Step 2 – *Clear the clutter from your mind.*** Too often, the world and its worries and priorities have crept in, taking up the space that God wants to occupy. You cannot develop that close relationship with Him if you are full of the world. We must reject and get rid of any strange fire that has crept in.

**Step 3 – *Fix your heart and mind on Him only.*** This is where your affection needs to be focused. (Colossians 3:2, KJV) This also means that you need to eliminate those things that will distract you from truly spending quality time with God.

**Step 4 – *Spend time in prayer.*** Communicate with the Lord. Use the Word as a starting point for your conversations. Worship Him through your prayers.

**Step 5 – *Wait on the Lord.*** After you have prayed, sit quietly and wait on Him to answer. When He speaks, thanksgiving will rise up within you because you have heard His voice. The tears may flow, but the joy of the Lord will be present. Praise and adoration will come (true worship), which will lead you right into His presence. It will be an exciting moment that you will never forget!

Preparation IS NOW! We cannot afford to wait any longer. As a bride does for her wedding day, we must prepare with the same intensity and dedication for the Bridegroom.

# The Destiny of True Worship

In Revelation 4:4-11, John paints a worship scene of what is to come at the end of the age:

*Around the throne were twenty-four thrones, and on the thrones I saw twenty-four elders sitting, clothed in white robes; and they had crowns of gold on their heads.*

*And from the throne proceeded lightnings, thunderings, and voices. Seven lamps of fire were burning before the throne, which are the seven Spirits of God.*

*Before the throne there was a sea of glass, like crystal. And in the midst of the throne, and around the throne, were four living creatures full of eyes in front and in back.*

*The first living creature was like a lion, the second living creature like a calf, the third living creature had a face like a man, and the fourth living creature was like a flying eagle.*

*The four living creatures, each having six wings, were full of eyes around and within. And they do not rest day or night, saying:*

*"Holy, holy, holy,*
*Lord God Almighty,*
*Who was and is and is to come!"*

*Whenever the living creatures give glory and honor and thanks to Him who sits on the throne, who lives forever and ever, the twenty-four elders fall down before Him who sits on the throne and worship Him who lives forever and ever, and cast their crowns before the throne saying,*

> *"You are worthy, O Lord,*
> *To receive glory and honor and power;*
> *For You created all things,*
> *And by Your will they exist and*
> *    were created."*

John continues in Revelation 5:11-14:

*"Then I looked, and I heard the voice of many angels around the throne, the living creatures, and the elders; and the number of them was ten thousand times ten thousand, and thousands of thousands, saying with a loud voice:*

> *"Worthy is the Lamb who was slain*
> *To receive power and riches*
> *    and wisdom,*
> *And strength and honor and glory*
> *    and blessing!"*

*And every creature which is in heaven and on the earth and under the earth and such as are in the sea, and all that are in them, I heard saying:*

*"Blessing and honor and glory*
  *and power*
*Be to Him who sits on the throne,*
*And to the Lamb forever and ever!"*

*Then the four living creatures said "Amen!" And the twenty-four elders fell down and worshiped Him who lives forever and ever.*

These passages demonstrate that God wants a people who are addicted to worship. He desires it, and He deserves it. Offering up true worship to the Lord is how the believer's forever story ends.

So, tell Him that you thirst for Him, you long for Him, and you desire Him. Seek His face in adoration and reverence. Cry out to the Lord. Make true worship your focus. This IS the destiny call upon your life.

I feel the presence of God right now! Let's take a praise and worship break...

Give Him all the glory and honor due His name. Shout, "Hallelujah!" Empty yourself before Him in complete adoration. Bow down and worship Him with all your heart. Yield your spirit to His Spirit in complete surrender.

Be like David in Psalms 42:1-2a and say:

> *As the deer pants for the water brooks, so my soul pants for You, O God. My soul thirsts for God, for the living God...*

Ask the Lord to create in you a heart for worship. Daily make the choice to rejoice only in Him. Continue to worship!

Soon, you will be in another realm, unaware of this world. You will experience Heaven on earth! You may start to weep but take care to quiet yourself and wait on Him to speak. He wants to reveal His heart to you, so let Him. Write down everything He says and keep a journal.

I pray that this type of worship experience becomes habitual for you. As Christ's bride, we need to practice His presence daily, for this is what it means to be a true worshiper. May you be transformed into a worship addict!

LET'S GO THERE!

# CHAPTER ELEVEN

## Final Thoughts

As believers, it is our absolute privilege to worship the Lord in spirit and in truth. Our worship must be pure and not tainted with strange fire. Being transformed into a true worshiper requires surrender, devotion, and a life fixated on Him.

Remember what I said in the last chapter? The life of the believer is about having an intimate relationship with the Lord. It is pursuing the heart of the Father, following His Son, and moving by the Spirit. It is all about living as true worshipers of the Most High God.

So, as we conclude our time together, I want to pray for you:

Father God,

In the name of Jesus, I pray that each and every reader of this book becomes hungry right now for Your presence and the power of God in their life. I pray that You will fill them, saturating them with Your unfailing love and Your everlasting well of joy.

I pray that they will come to know who they really are in You. I pray that their minds are renewed and re-programmed for the transcendent life of glory that is available to all true worshipers. I pray that Your wisdom will cause them to flourish, excel, and be victorious in all things.

I pray that You will birth within them an eagerness and a heart-felt yearning to spend intimate time with You. Hover over them, Holy Spirit. Show them great and mighty things. I pray that You will inject them with spiritual vitamins that will make them spiritually healthy and boost their appetites for the Word of God. I pray that they will come to know that Your presence is both an internal and external reality. I pray that fresh oil will be poured upon them as they daily surrender to You.

Circumcise the hearts of pastors, ministers, worship leaders, singers, and praise teams as they lead Your people in worshiping You. I pray that they will desire more of You and more of Your anointed and fresh oil. Let Your fire fall upon these, Your servants. I pray that You, Lord, will be magnified in their lives. I thank You for the privilege to pray for these, my fellow servants in the ministry of Jesus Christ.

I pray all this in the name that is above all names, Jesus Christ our Lord. Amen!

Enjoy your journey as a true worshiper of our great and mighty God!

Love,

Minister Patricia Taylor

# Afterword

# The Way to Salvation

I want to take a moment here to address those of you who have not yet accepted Jesus Christ as your personal Savior. If this book has touched your life in any way, and you desire to have an intimate relationship with the Lord, I want to invite you to receive Him right now. He loves you unconditionally and cares about all the things that concern you. In fact, He loved you so much that He gave His life for you by dying on the cross.

Romans 5:8 says:

*But God demonstrates His own love toward us, in that while we were still sinners, Christ died for us.*

The greatest miracle is not physical but spiritual. Only the Savior can give you the gift of salvation. So, even though it is essential to be saved or born again, get your mind off the process of "being saved" and focus on the actual person of the Savior. In other words, you cannot bypass the person of Jesus Christ in order to reach Heaven.

As John 1:12 tells us:

*But as many as received Him, to them He gave the right to become children of God, to those who believe in His name:*

So, receive Him by faith in your heart. All you have to do is say YES to Him, believe in the work of the cross, and take a hold of the salvation that is freely given you. Also, if you have read this book, and you are not sure of your salvation or have fallen away from a previous commitment, you, too, can receive His gift of salvation right now.

Please pray the following prayer from the heart:

Heavenly Father,

I come to You in the name of Jesus. Your Word says, *"that whosoever shall call on the name of the Lord shall be saved."* (Acts 2:21, KJV) I am calling on You. I pray and ask Jesus to come into my heart and be Lord over my life according to Romans 10:9 which states that *"if* [I] *confess with* [my] *mouth the Lord Jesus and believe in* [my] *heart that God has raised Him from the dead,* [I] *will be saved."* I do that now. I confess that Jesus is Lord, and I believe in my heart that God died on the cross for my sin and raised Him from the dead.

I am now reborn! I am a Christian—a child of the Almighty God! I am saved! Thank you, Father! In Jesus' name. Amen.

Shout, "Hallelujah!" This is a great day of celebration and the first step to becoming a true worshiper of the Most High.

Welcome to the Family of God!

# About the Author

In 1998, Patricia Taylor accepted her call into the ministry of the Gospel. Since then, she has been sharing the Word as well as serving through her singing ministry. With a burning passion for worship, she is known as an anointed psalmist and has often been called "The Voice."

Patricia has traveled throughout the U.S.A. and Europe, worshiping God through her voice. She has led worship and ministered in song at her home church, as part of Pastor Benny Hinn's ministry, and elsewhere. She has preached the Word of God in numerous churches as well as to women on skid row and to their children. Today, she is teaching and preaching the Word on social media platforms as well as in person. She continues to be available to minister, either through the Word or in song.

Using her life as an example, Minister Taylor illustrates the importance of being prepared for the work of the ministry in these last days. Her zeal to walk as a true worshiper of the Most High fuels her message that calls the Church to live an authentic life of worship before God.

Patricia is a native of Los Angeles, California. She has two children, five grandchildren, and one great-grandson.

If you wish to book her to speak or to minister in song, please contact her at: **patriciataylorministries@gmail.com**

You can also visit her website at: **patriciataylorministries.org**

# Endnotes

[i] Bynum, Juanita. "The Golden Altar of Incense – Prayer – Part 13." *Essence of God: Oilofthespirit's Weblog,* 16 November 2008. https://oilofthespirit.wordpress.com/2008/11/16/the-golden-altar-of-incense-prayer-part-13/